MISSIONARY'S LITTLE BOOK
of
Inspirational Stories

compiled by

R. DALE & V. RUTH JEFFERY

Covenant Communications, Inc.

Cover photo © PhotoDisc, Inc.

Published by Covenant Communications, Inc.
American Fork, Utah

Printed in the United States of America
First Printing: February 2000

06 05 04 03 02   10 9 8 7 6 5

ISBN 1-57734-606-8

This book is dedicated to missionaries, young and old, full-time and member, serving around the world to bring the restored gospel to those waiting to hear. "Let your light so shine before men, that they may see your good works, and glorify your Father which is in heaven" (Matthew 5:16).

PREFACE

Over twelve years and two missions, we have collected thoughts, stories, and poems that inspire and illustrate gospel principles. Although some of these stories may appear to have been based on actual events, in their present form, they should be viewed as inspiring stories rather than factual accounts.

We thank the original authors for their inspiring words, and apologize for any attribution errors or omissions.

Stories have been edited for clarity.

We welcome comments and contributions. Please contact us at **RuthnDale@excite.com**.

—R. Dale and V. Ruth Jeffery

Dale and Ruth Jeffery and their two sons have recently been serving a two-year stake mission in the Maplewood III (Chinese-speaking) Branch in Houston Texas.

ATTITUDE

FAITH

GOALS AND HABITS

HARD WORK

LEADERSHIP

LOVE AND SERVICE

MISSIONARY WORK

OBEDIENCE

OUR SAVIOR JESUS CHRIST

OVERCOMING OBSTACLES

PRAYER

PROPHETS

SCRIPTURES

ATTITUDE

It's your attitude,
not your aptitude,
that determines your altitude in life.

As a Man Thinketh . . .

A wise man stood at the gate of an ancient city and greeted travelers as they arrived. One day, a traveler asked him:

"What kind of people live in this city?"

The wise man responded with a question of his own: "What kind of people lived in the city from whence you came?"

"Oh, they were very bad people," answered the traveler, "cruel, deceitful, and devil-worshipping."

"You'll find the same kind of people in this city," sighed the wise man.

Some time later, a second traveler came to the gate and asked about the people in the city. The wise man again asked his question:

"What kind of people lived in the city from whence you came?"

"Oh, they were very good people," answered the second traveler, "hard-working, generous, and God-fearing."

"You'll find the same kind of people in this city," smiled the wise man.

– AS TOLD BY KIMBERLY EVANS JONES

Word of Honor

"My friends, I have been asked what is meant by 'word of honor.' I will tell you. Place me behind prison walls—high, thick walls of stone. It is possible that somehow I could escape. But stand me on the floor, draw a chalk line around me and have me give my word of honor not to cross it and I would never cross the line. I'd die first!"

– KARL G. MAESER

Self-Possession

I walked with my friend to the newsstand the other night. He bought a paper and thanked the newsie politely. The newsie didn't even acknowledge him.

"A sullen fellow, isn't he?" I commented.

"Oh, he's that way every night," shrugged my friend.

"Then why do you continue to be so polite to him?" I asked.

"Why not?" inquired my friend. "Why should I let him decide how I'm going to act?"

As I thought about this incident, it occurred to me that the important word my friend used was "act." My friend acts, while most of us react to people. He has a sense of inner balance most of us lack. He knows who he is, what he stands for, and how he should behave. He refuses to return incivility for incivility, because he controls his own conduct.

We must become masters of our own actions and attitudes. To let another person determine whether we will be rude or gracious, elated or depressed, is to give up control of ourselves. The only true possession is self-possession.

– SYDNEY J. HARRIS

Two Buckets

Two buckets were sitting on the edge of a well. One turned to the other with mouth drooping down, "All I do is go down and come up and go down and come up all day long. No matter how many times I come up full, I always go down empty."

The other bucket gave a warm smile." That's funny," she said." I do the same thing. All I do is go down and come up and go down and come up all day long. But no matter how many times I go down empty, I always come up full."

– BITS AND PIECES

Look to This Day!

Look to this day!
For it is life, the very life of life.
In its brief course lie all the varieties and realities
of your existence:
The bliss of growth;
The glory of action;
The splendor of beauty;
For yesterday is already a dream, and tomorrow is
only a vision;
But today, well lived, makes every yesterday
A dream of happiness, and every tomorrow a
vision of hope.
Look well, therefore, to this day.

– FROM THE SANSKRIT

A Tale of Two Frogs

Two frogs fell into a deep milk bowl.
One of them had an optimist's soul,
While the other took a gloomier view:
"We shall drown," he cried, without further adieu,
And with one last despairing cry,
He flung up his legs and said goodbye.

Said the other frog with a merry grin,
"I can't get out, but I won't give in;
I'll keep swimming around till my strength is spent,
Then at least I'll die the more content."

So bravely he swam, until it would seem,
His struggles began to churn the cream.
And on top of the butter at last, he stopped—
then out of the bowl he gaily hopped.
What of the moral? It's easily found:
If you cannot hop out, keep swimming around.

– ANTHONY P. CASTLE

The Drug Store

A few months after moving to a small town, a woman complained to a neighbor about the poor service at the local drug store. She hoped the neighbor would repeat her complaint to the store's owner.

The next time she went to the drugstore the druggist greeted her with a big smile and told her how happy he was to see her again. He said he hoped she liked their town and to please let him know if there was anything he could do to help her get settled. He then filled her order promptly and courteously.

Later the woman reported the miraculous change to her friend. "I suppose you told the druggist how poor I thought the service was?" she asked.

"Actually," the woman said. "I told him you were amazed at the way he had built up his drug store and you thought it was one of the best you'd ever seen."

– AUTHOR UNKNOWN

The Man Who Thinks He Can

If you think you are beaten, you are;
If you think you dare not, you don't.
If you like to win, but think you can't;
It's almost a cinch you won't.

If you think you'll lose, your lost.
For out in the world we find,
Success begins with a fellow's will;
It's all in the state of mind.

If you think you are outclassed, you are;
You've got to think high to rise.
You've got to be sure of yourself before
You can ever win the prize.

Life's battles don't always go
To the stronger and faster man;
But sooner or later the man who wins
Is the man who thinks he can.

– WALTER D. WINGLE

Perspective

After the great London fire in 1066, the great English architect, Sir Christopher Wren, volunteered his services to plan and build one of the world's greatest cathedrals. Often, he would walk among the workers, watching the construction. One day, he asked three stonecutters what they were doing.

One of them answered, "I am cutting this stone."

Another answered, "I am earning my three shillings per day."

The third stood up, squared his shoulders and proudly said, "I am helping Sir Christopher Wren build a magnificent cathedral."

– THE SCOUTER'S MINUTE

You Become What You Think

You know you sometimes think yourself into unhappiness and depression. But did you know, you could also think yourself into happiness? By positive thinking, you will be well, you will prosper, and your prayers will be answered. Become the master of your thoughts. Stop thinking about how tough life is, stop thinking about the future and the past, think of God's riches and love, and express these thoughts daily. You will become what you think.

– ALBERT E. CLIFFE

Ten Steps to a Joyful and Enthusiastic Life

Since thinking has much to do with what you become in life, you might consider the following suggestions:

First: Stop putting yourself down. There is a lot that is good in you. Empty your mind of thoughts of failure and start seeing yourself as a competent person.

Second: Eliminate self-pity. Think of what you have, instead of dwelling on what you may have lost.

Third: Quit thinking about yourself. Think of others. Go out and look for someone who needs the help you can give, and give it freely.

Fourth: Remember the words of Goethe: "He who has a firm will molds the world to himself." God gave humans something called will. Use it.

Fifth: Have a goal and set an achievable timetable to achieve it.

Sixth: Stop wasting your mental energy on the past, and start thinking about what to do now. Amazing things happen when you think constructively.

Seventh: Every morning and every evening say these words aloud: "I can do all things through Christ who strengthens me."

Eighth: Every day say three times: "This is the day the Lord has made. I will rejoice and be glad in it" (adapted from Psalms 118:24).

Ninth: Think and practice joy every day.

Tenth: Get enthusiasm; think enthusiasm; live enthusiastically!

– NORMAL VINCENT PEALE

FAITH

And Jesus said unto them . . . If ye have faith as a grain of mustard seed, ye shall say unto this mountain, Remove hence to yonder place; and it shall remove; and nothing shall be impossible unto you.

– MATTHEW 17:20

For the brother of Jared said unto the mountain Zerin, Remove—and it was removed. And if he had not had faith it would not have moved.

– ETHER 12:30

Wings

Be like the bird, who,
Halting in his flight,
On limb too slight,
Feels it give way beneath him,
Yet sings,
Knowing he hath wings.

– VICTOR HUGO

Faith and Works

A man hired a young boy, whose father owned a small boat, to row him across a lake. About halfway across the man noticed a "W" painted on one oar and an "F" on the other. When he asked what the letters meant, he was told that F stood for FAITH and W stood for WORKS. If you just row with faith, you go in circles to your left," said the boy. "If you row only with works, you go in circles to your right. In order to go straight ahead you have to use both of them."

The same principle applies to life. If we just use faith, or only works, we will go in circles. We must use both to make progress.

– RETOLD BY JOHN QUINLAN

Faith

It is faith that bridges the land of breath
To the realms of the souls departed,
That comforts the living in days of death,
And strengthens the heavy-hearted.
It is faith in his dreams that keeps a man
Face front to the odds about him,
And he shall conquer who thinks he can,
In spite of the throngs who doubt him.
Each must stand in the court of life
And pass through the hours of trial;
He shall be tested by the rules of strife,
And tried for his self-denial.
Time shall bruise his soul with the loss of friends,
And frighten him with disaster;
But he shall find when the anguish ends
That, of all things, faith is master.
So keep your faith in the God above,
And faith in the righteous truth,
It shall bring you back to the absent love,
And the joys of a vanished youth.

You shall smile once more when your tears are dried,
meet trouble and swiftly rout it,
For faith is the strength of the soul inside,
And lost is the man without it.

– EDGAR A. GUEST

The Pathway to Success

Opportunity knocked upon the door
and Wonder said, "Who's there?"
Courage went out to let him in
For he had many things to share.
Caution then asked him to explain
The things he had for us.
Interest intuited the nature of
the business to discuss.
Logic debated where and when
that this could and should be done.
Decision then decided who
and Knowledge emerged as the one.
Hope and Ambition added bits
as they conferred apart,
but Faith just turned her smiling face
and said, "When do we start?"

– FROM THE MTC SISTERS' MEETING NOTES, 1988

Love and Faith

Where there is no faith, there can be no love. Love, like faith, demands confidence without assurance. As with all things spiritual, there can be no certitude, for faith goes beyond reason and evidence, and love is above even these.

If we need them, there are many simple proofs of the existence of love in our daily lives: we plant a seed and it becomes a flower; we touch someone and they grow in strength; we wipe away tears and learn to smile again.

We begin to be comfortable with love only when, deep in our hearts, we fully accept its reality. Love hasn't a chance if we are forever questioning it or requiring it to be validated. Pascal said, "faith is different from proof; the latter is human, the former is from God."

– LEO S. BUSCAGLIA, PhD

Faith

I will not doubt, though all my ships at sea
Come drifting home with broken masts and sails;
I shall believe the Hand that never fails,
For seeming evil worketh good to me;
And, though I weep because those sails are
    battered,
Still will I cry, while my best hopes lie shattered,
"I trust in Thee."
I will not doubt, though all my prayers return
Unanswered from the still, white realm above;
I shall believe it is an all-wise Love
That has refused those things for which I yearn;
And though, at times, I cannot keep from
    grieving,
Yet the pure ardor of my fixed believing
Undimmed shall burn.
I will not doubt, though sorrows fall like rain,
And troubles swarm like bees about a hive;
I shall believe the heights for which I strive,
Are only reached by anguish and by pain;

And, though I groan and tremble with my
    crosses,
I yet shall see, through my severest losses,
The greater gain.
I will not doubt; well anchored in the faith,
Like some staunch ship, my soul braves every
    gale,
So strong its courage that it will not fail
To breast the mighty, unknown sea of death.
Oh, may I cry when body parts with spirit,
"I do not doubt," so listening worlds may hear it
With my last breath.

– ELLA WHEELER WILCOX

He's with Me

Storm clouds and strong gusts of wind had come up suddenly over Columbus, Ohio. The Alpine Elementary School radio blared tornado warnings. It was too dangerous to send the children home. Instead, they were taken to the basement, where the children huddled together in fear.

The teachers were worried too. To help ease the tension, the principal suggested a sing-along. But the voices were weak and unenthusiastic. Child after child began to cry—we could not calm them.

Then a teacher, whose faith seemed equal to any emergency, whispered to the child closest to her, "Aren't you forgetting something, Kathie? There is a power greater than the storm that will protect us. Just say to yourself, 'God is with me now.' Then pass the words on to the child next to you."

As these words were whispered from child to child, a sense of peace settled over the group. I could hear the wind outside blowing with the same ferocity as before, but it didn't seem to matter.

Inside, fear subsided and tears faded away.

When the all-clear signal came over the radio, students and staff returned to their classrooms.

Through the years I have remembered those calming words. In times of stress and trouble, I have been able to find release from fear or tension by repeating, "God is with me now."

– PHYLLIS I. MARTIN

GOALS AND HABITS

No life ever grows great
until it is focused, dedicated, and disciplined.
– HENRY EMERSON FOSDICK

Habits

We first form habits; then habits form us. As we reach for success, if we do not consciously form good habits we will unconsciously form bad ones.

It's just as easy to form the habit of succeeding as it is to succumb to the habit of failure.

Habits aren't instincts; they're acquired reactions. They don't just happen; they are caused. Once you determine the cause of a habit, you have the power to accept or reject it.

It is a psychological fact that you can influence your environment and thoughts. If you do so consciously and with high purpose, you can change your habits and attitudes for the better.

To know the true reality of yourself, you must be aware of both your conscious thoughts and your unconscious prejudices, biases and habits.

Every person who has become successful has formed the habit of doing things failures dislike doing and will not do.

Anyone can live heroically and successfully for one day. The man who achieves a high purpose makes that day the pattern for all the days of his life.

Fear is a habit; so are self-pity, defeat, anxiety, despair, hopelessness and resignation. You can eliminate all of these negative habits with two simple resolves: "I can!" and "I will!"

Good work habits help develop an internal toughness and a self-confident attitude that will sustain you through every adversity and temporary discouragement.

The harvest we reap in our lives is measured by the attitudes and habits we cultivate.

– PAUL J. MEYER

The Farmer's Son

There once was a farmer. He was proud of his work, and always had straight, long rows of corn, wheat, and all manner of healthy crops.

When the farmer's son was old enough to learn the farm work, the farmer took him out into the fields to teach him how to hoe, plant seeds, irrigate, and other small chores. One day, the farmer decided his son was old enough to learn how to plow. He put him on a tractor and told him how to plow straight, long furrows. The way to do this, he said, was to set your sight on something on the opposite side of the field, and to steer straight toward it, not veering to one side or the other.

The farmer then went off to other chores. When he came back to check his son's work, he was dismayed to find the field full of crooked rows. He was furious! He stormed over to the tractor to find out the reason for this foolishness.

The son explained, "Well, Dad, I did just what you said. I sighted in on something on the opposite side of the field, and headed straight for it. I never veered to one side or the other."

"Then why are the rows going every which way?"

"Well, the darn cow kept moving!"

– RETOLD BY LARRY S. JEFFERY

Boiling The Frog

There is an old saying that you can't kill a frog by dropping it into hot water. A frog dropped into hot water will immediately jump out. But if you put the frog in cold water and gradually warm it up until it is scalding hot, you will have him cooked before he knows it.

The encroachment of bad habits in our lives is very much like this. They seem rather small things at first—things we do or say that at first seem trivial. But once we are lulled away in false beliefs and self-denial, the Devil can turn up the heat. Until our frog, so to speak, is cooked.

– RETOLD BY DENISE MARTINEZ

How to Catch a Monkey

In India, people catch monkeys by setting out a small box with a tasty nut in it. There is an opening in the box—large enough for the monkey to put in his empty hand, but too small for him to pull it out once he grabs the nut. Once the monkey has the nut, he must let go to regain his freedom. If he keeps holding the nut, he is trapped.

Most monkeys will not let go of the nut, making it easy for hunters to catch them.

People have been known to be caught in similar traps—the prize in the box controls us—but we can free ourselves if we are willing to let go.

– ELIZABETH BRENNER

The Winds of Fate

One ship drives east and another drives west,
with the self-same winds that blow.
'Tis the set of the sails,
and not the gales,
that tells us the way to go.

Like the winds of the sea are the ways of fate,
as we voyage along through life;
'tis the set of the soul
that decides its goal,
and not the calm or the strife.

– ELLA WHEELER WILCOX

Begin Where You Are

The greatest thing in this world is not so much where we stand as in what direction we are moving. To reach the port of heaven, we must sail sometimes with the wind and sometimes against it. But we must sail, and not drift nor lie at anchor.

– OLIVER WENDELL HOLMES

Press On!

Follow your dream.
Take one step at a time
And don't settle for less,
Just continue to climb.

Follow your dream.
If you stumble don't stop
And lose sight of your goal,
Press on to the top!

For only on top
Can we see the whole view—
Can we see what we've done
And what we can do—
Can we then have the vision
To seek something new.
Press on,
And follow your dream!

– AMANDA BRADLEY

The Back Fence

There was a little boy with a bad temper. His father gave him a bag of nails and told him that every time he lost his temper, to hammer a nail in the back fence.

By the end of the first day the boy had driven 37 nails into the fence. Over time, the boy decided it was easier to hold his temper than to drive nails into fence posts.

Finally, a day came when the boy didn't lose his temper. When he told his father, he congratulated him, and told the boy to pull out one nail each day he didn't lose his temper. Weeks passed and one day the young boy told his father that all the nails were gone. The father took his son by the hand and led him to the fence.

"You have done well, my son, but look at the holes. The fence will never be the same. When you say things in anger, they leave scars just like these. A verbal wound is as bad as a physical one."

– GENA WILLIAMSON

12 Points to Perpetual Happiness

1. **Understand that being happy is an emotional decision**, just as anger, pride, and repentance are emotional decisions. Decide now that you will work at being happy more often. You are either the master of your destiny or a slave to your fate. Only you can choose how you'll react to a situation. Choose well.

2. **Always associate with people who will lift you up.** There are people everywhere who will tell you how bad things are and how you'll never amount to anything. These people are really talking about themselves. You should find better company.

3. **Meet everybody on friendly terms.** Each new person could be your next best friend, or the person who will pull you out of a ditch in half an hour. Treat them as such.

4. **You become what you think about and tell yourself all day.** Safeguard your thoughts, and when you talk to yourself, say positive things.

5. **Keep yourself too busy to mope around.** Sitting around with I, Me, Mine and Myself (your four worst friends) and bemoaning your existence will get you nowhere. Keep your day full of people and projects and family and correspondence. Advance every day in the direction of your goals.

6. **Be involved in big projects** to help you organize yourself, and your time. I'm continually amazed at how much more I can get done (in my spare time) when I work 75 hours a week than when I work 20.

7. **Cultivate humor always, but cynicism never.** Laughing at yourself and chuckling at the humor in your situation keeps you from taking yourself too seriously and wanting to strangle somebody. Picking on other people doesn't lift them up, and it doesn't help you up either.

8. **Read 15 minutes' worth of inspirational material before noon every day.** This not only lifts your spirit and marks the path before you, but also gives you something good to talk about

9. **Memorize words of upbeat songs and inspirational quotes**. Keep these on hand when you have nothing else to think about.

10. **Opinions change—facts remain the same.** Learn to separate opinion from fact, and don't get caught up in anybody's opinion, even your own. Especially, don't live your life based on what other people might think about you.

11. **Don't worry about things you have no control over.** Learn to solve problems quickly. Learn to anticipate, work through, or avoid the things (problems) you can't solve. Plan ahead, and don't forget to make a "Plan B."

12. **Keep your faith in God and in the Big Picture.** Even though you can't see all the curves in the road ahead, be confident that things will straighten themselves out (with your help) eventually. If you are doing your part you can have every expectation that God will do His part.

– R. DALE JEFFERY

The Starfish

An old man was walking along the beach. In the distance he saw someone who seemed to be dancing along the waves. As he got closer, he saw a young man picking up starfish and tossing them back into the ocean.

"What are you doing? The old man asked.

"The sun is coming up and the tide is going out. If I don't throw them in they will die."

"But young man, there are miles and miles of beach with starfish all along it. You can't possibly make a difference."

The young man bent down, picked up a starfish and threw it back past the breaking waves. "It made a difference to that one."

The young man's actions represent something in each of us. We are all gifted with the ability to make a difference. Each of us can shape our own future, and each of us can help others reach their potential.

Vision without action is merely a dream.
Action without vision just passes time.
Vision with action can change the world!
– AUTHOR UNKNOWN

HARD WORK

It is only those
who do not know how to work
that do not love it.
To those who do,
it is better than play.

— JOHN MASON BROWN

Strive

It's the steady, constant driving
To the goal for which you're striving,
Not the speed that you travel
That will make the victory sure.
It's the everlasting gaining,
Without a whimper or complaining
At the burdens you are bearing,
Or the woes you must endure.
It's the holding to a purpose
And the never giving in;
It's the cutting down the distance
By the little that you win.
It's the iron will to do it
And the steady sticking to it.
So, whate'er your task, go to it
And life's purpose you will win.

– AUTHOR UNKNOWN

It Couldn't Be Done

Somebody said that it couldn't be done,
But he with a chuckle replied,
"Maybe it couldn't," but he would be one
Who wouldn't say so till he tried.
So he buckled right in with the trace of a grin
On his face. If he worried, he hid it.
He started to sing as he tackled the thing
That couldn't be done, and he did it!
Somebody scoffed: "Oh, you'll never do that;
At least no one ever has done it;"
But he took off his coat and he took off his hat,
And the first thing we knew he'd begun it,
With a lift of his chin and a bit of a grin,
Without any doubting or quiddit,
He started to sing as he tackled the thing
That couldn't be done, and he did it!
There are thousands to tell you it cannot be done,
There are thousands to prophesy failure;
There are thousands to point out to you, one by one,
The dangers that await to assail you.
But just buckle in with a bit of a grin,

45

Just take off your coat and go to it;
Just start to sing as you tackle the thing
That "cannot be done," and you'll do it!

– EDGAR A. GUEST

If You Want A Thing Bad Enough

If you want a thing bad enough
To go out and fight for it,
Work day and night for it,
Give up your time and your peace and your sleep for it,
If only desire of it makes you mad enough never
  to tire of it—
Makes you give up all things tawdry and cheap
  for it—
If life seems all useless and empty without it,
And all that you scheme and you dream is about it,
If gladly you'll sweat for it,
Fret for it, plan for it,
Lose all your terror of devils or man for it,
If you'll simply go after the thing you want
With all your capacity, strength and sagacity
Faith, hope, and confidence, stern pertinacity,
If neither cold, poverty, famine, nor gaunt
Nor sickness nor pain of body and brain
Can keep you away from the thing that you want,
If dogged and grim you besiege and beset it,
You'll get it!

– AUTHOR UNKNOWN

The Parable of the Popping Corn

Behold, at the time of harvest, the ears of corn did bring forth kernels, which were dried and prepared for the popper's hand. And then it was that the popper did take the kernels, all of which did appear alike unto him, and did apply the oil and the heat.

And lo, it came to pass that when the heat was on, some did explode with promise and did magnify themselves an hundred fold, and some did burst forth with whiteness that did both gladden the eye and satisfy the taste of the popper. And likewise some others did also pop, but not too much.

But lo, there were some that did just lie there and even though the popper's heat was alike unto all, they did bask in the warmth of the oil and kept everything they had for themselves. And so it came to pass that those that had kept of the warmth, yea, and did not burst forth, were fit only to be cast out into the trash pail, to be thought of with hardness and disgust.

And thus we see that in the beginning all appear alike, but when the heat is on, some come forth and give their all, while others fail to pop and verily become like unto chaff, to be discarded and forgotten.

– WILLIAM JAMES MORTIMER

The Stonecutter

Long ago there lived a stonecutter who every morning took his tools to the mountainside where he cut and polished slabs of rock for wealthy homes. He was very good at his work, and he was happy. But one day, as he carried a finely polished block of stone to the house of a rich man, he saw many beautiful things that he never had seen before.

"Oh!" he cried. "I wish I were rich. I wish I might sleep in a bed as soft as down. "Then he picked up his tools and started home, but the spirit of the mountain had heard his wish. Instead of the poor little hut he had left in the morning, there stood a wonderful palace full of beautiful furniture. The stonecutter slept that night on a bed as soft as down. When he awoke, he looked out his new window to enjoy the beautiful morning. As he stood there, a fine carriage rolled past drawn by snow-white horses. The prince's servants were running in front and behind the carriage and the prince was sitting inside with a golden canopy over his head. The stonecutter again was disappointed and discontented.

"Oh!" he said." I wish I were a prince with a carriage and a golden canopy."

No sooner had he wished, than it came to pass. He was a prince; he had servants dressed in purple and gold and he drove through the streets in his carriage. For a while he was happy, but one day he noticed that the sun was drying and wilting his grass and flowers even though he had watered them only hours before.

"The sun is mightier than I am. I wish to be the sun."

The spirit heard him and the stonecutter was changed to the sun.

He felt proud and mighty being so great and yellow in the sky. He burned the fields of rich and poor alike. But one day a cloud covered his face; again he was filled with discontent.

"The cloud is mightier than I. I would be the cloud," he cried.

So the mountain spirit changed him into a cloud and he lay content for a while between the sun and the earth. He caught the sunbeams and would not let them go. He sent rain to earth and the flowers bloomed, but this was not enough. He began pouring down rain until the rivers overflowed and the crops were ruined. He washed away whole towns; but try as he would, the one thing he could not move was the mountain.

"The mountain is stronger than I. I will be the mountain."

At once the mountain spirit changed him into rock. For years he stood, proudly raising his head above the other cliffs, and he did not feel the sun or the rain. But one day he heard a sharp tap tapping and he saw a stonecutter working with his sharp tools, cutting into his side.

"Who can cut into me? I would be that Man."

So once again, the man became a stonecutter. He lived in a hut and worked from morning to night. Yet he was happy for he had learned that a steady tap tapping moves mountains.

– A JAPANESE LEGEND

The Minister's Crop

The story is told about a minister in Africa who called the natives to him one day and asked them to help him harvest his grain. He asked each of them to bring a basket to carry the grain to the market in town. The market was about 5 kilometers away, and each worker had to make several trips to get the crop to market. Some of the natives came as a sign of thanks to the minister. Others brought their entire families so all could help. Others, however, dragged themselves out with slothful hearts and the smallest baskets they could find.

At the end of the day, the minister let each worker fill his basket for himself as a wage. Those who had brought big baskets had a great store of grain. But those who had purposely brought small baskets so they wouldn't have to work as hard were disappointed to find that their reward was equal to their desire to help.

– AUTHOR UNKNOWN

Stick to Your Task

Stick to your task 'til it sticks to you;
Beginners are many, but enders are few.
Honor, power, place and praise
Will come, in time, to the one who stays.
Stick to your task 'til it sticks to you;
Bend at it, sweat at it, smile at it too;
For out of the bend and the sweat and the smile
Will come life's victories after awhile.

– AUTHOR UNKNOWN

The Secret of Achievement

It took Michelangelo twelve years—one brush stoke at a time—to paint his Biblical scenes in the Sistine Chapel. It took Brahms twenty years—one note at a time—to compose his First Symphony. It took Edmund Hillary and Tenzing Norgay eighty days—one step at a time—to climb the 29,000 feet of Mount Everest.

Word by word, brush-stroke by brush-stroke, note by note, step by step, problem by problem, prayer by prayer—this is the secret of achievement.

– AUTHOR UNKNOWN

Hard Work

There are moments when things go well, and one feels encouraged. There are difficult moments, and one feels overwhelmed. But it is senseless to speak of optimism or pessimism. The important thing to know is that if one works well in a potato field, the potatoes will grow. If one works well among men, they will grow. That's reality. The rest is smoke.

– DANILO DOLCI

The Champion

The average runner sprints
Until the breath in him is gone;
But the champion has the iron will:
That makes him carry on.

For rest, the average runner begs,
When limp his muscles grow;
But the champion runs on leaden legs
His spirit makes him go.

The average man's complacent
When he does his best to score;
But the champion does his best
And then he does a little more.

– AUTHOR UNKNOWN

The Ant and the Grasshopper

All through the warm days of summer, a green grasshopper hopped happily among the flowers. When he was thirsty, he sipped nectar from the closest blossom. One afternoon, as the grasshopper was leaping from flower to flower, he saw beneath him a little black ant struggling to carry a fat leaf bigger than himself. "Little friend," said the grasshopper, "what are you doing down there?"

"Why, I am carrying this leaf off to my nest. I must fill my nest with food to last through winter."

"Winter?" said the grasshopper. "Who cares about winter? Why don't you climb up to this flower and enjoy its sweet nectar? Winter will take care of itself."

"That isn't the way things work in this world," said the ant. "Winter will be here soon. The flowers will be gone, and there will be nothing to eat."

"Well, suit yourself," said the grasshopper.

And off he went, singing happily and carefree.

The ant returned to his work. It took all his strength to carry each morsel of food, but he did not mind. He knew he would be ready for winter.

Soon the cold weather came. The ant was snug in his nest with plenty of food. The grasshopper? He had nothing, and soon was no more.

A WISE PERSON KNOWS THAT SUMMER DOES NOT LAST FOREVER.

— AESOP

LEADERSHIP

Do not go where the path may lead.
Go instead where there is no path,
And blaze a trail.

– ANONYMOUS

Leadership

A great leader suffers in a hundred different ways,
and keeps his suffering to himself.

A great leader loves being alone with God.

A great leader overcomes himself, rises above
himself, every day, every minute.

A great leader is polite, but he never tones down
the truth just to please others.

A great leader hitches his wagon to the remote,
the unattainable, the stars.

A great leader is very simple, but the moral force
of his conviction shines through every tone of
his voice and every gesture of his hand.

A great leader is absolutely fearless—fearless
because he fears only God.

A great leader loves, not sentimentally, not by
making an effort, but with the effortless over
flow of God's love for him.

A great leader is decisive, yet with the utmost
tentativeness and tenderness.

You insult a great leader if you call him great; he does not want your judgment; he works and lives only to please God.

– CHARLES H. MALIK

Beacons of Light

Do all things without murmurings and disputings: That ye may be blameless and harmless, the sons of God, without rebuke, in the midst of a crooked and perverse nation, among whom ye shine as lights in the world.

– PHILIPPIANS 2:14-15

Outwitted

He drew a circle that shut me out—
Heretic, rebel, a thing to flout.
But Love and I had the wit to win:
We drew a circle that took him in.

– EDWIN MARKHAM

My Chum

He stood at the crossroads all alone,
The sunlight in his face.
He had no thought for the world unknown—
He was set for a manly race.
But the roads stretched east and the roads
   stretched west,
And the lad knew not which road was best,
So he chose the road that led him down,
And he lost the race and the victor's crown.
He was caught at last in an angry snare,
Because no one stood at the crossroads there
To show him the better road.
Another day at the self-same place,
A boy with high hopes stood.
He, too, was set for a manly race;
He, too, sought the things that were good.
But one was there who the roads did know,
And that one showed him which way to go.
So he turned from the road that would lead him
   down,

And he won the race and the victor's crown.
He walks today the highway fair
Because one stood at the crossroads there
To show him the better way.

– ANONYMOUS

The Eye's a Better Student

The eye's a better student and more willing than
    the ear.
Fine counsel is confusing, but example's always clear,
And the best of all the preachers are the men who
    live their creeds,
For to see the good in action is what everybody
    needs.
I can soon learn how you do it, if you'll let me see
    it done.
I can watch your hands in action, but your
    tongue too fast may run;
And the lectures you deliver may be wise and true,
But I'd rather get my lesson by observing what
    you do.
For I may not understand you and the high
    advice you give;
But there's no misunderstanding how you act and
    how you live.

– EDGAR A. GUEST

Discovery

There is no greater or more satisfying reward than that which comes from discovering and developing men. The possibilities are almost unlimited. Talent, like oil, is discovered in unexpected places and in surprising quantities.

– A.A. STAMBAUGH

True Nobility

Who does his task from day to day
And meets whatever comes his way,
Believing God has willed it so,
Has found real greatness here below
Who guards his post, no matter where,
Believing God must need him there,
Although but lowly toil it be,
Has risen to nobility.
For great and low there's but one test;
'Tis that each man shall do his best.
Who works with all the strength he can
Shall never die in debt to man.

— EDGAR A. GUEST

African Cedars

A British colonial administrator in Africa rode out one day to inspect a section of land that had been devastated by a storm. At one point he came to a place where giant cedars had been uprooted and destroyed.

He said to his official in charge of forestry, "You will have to plant some cedars here."

The official replied, "It takes two hundred years to grow cedars the size these were. They don't even bear cones until they are fifty years old."

"Then," said the administrator, "we must plant them at once!"

– THE SCOUTER'S MINUTE

Get Ahead

Our business in life is not to get ahead of others but to get ahead of ourselves; to break our own records; to outstrip our yesterdays by our todays; to bear our trials more beautifully than we ever dreamed we could; to give as we never have given; to do our work with more force and a finer finish than ever. This is the true goal: to get ahead of ourselves.

– CARL HOLMES

The Seagulls

In our friendly neighbor city of St. Augustine, great flocks of seagulls are starving amid plenty. Fishing is good, but the gulls don't know how to fish. For generations they have depended on the shrimp fleet to toss them scraps from their nets.

And now the fleet has moved.

The shrimpers over the years had created a "welfare state" for the seagulls. The birds never bothered to learn how to fish for themselves, and they never taught their children to fish. Instead, they led their little ones to the shrimp boats for their food.

Now the seagulls, the fine free birds that almost symbolize liberty itself, are starving to death because they gave in to the "something-for-nothing" lure! They sacrificed their independence for a handout.

Let's not be gullible gulls. We must preserve our talents of self-sufficiency, our genius for creating things for ourselves, our sense of thrift and our true love of independence.

– FROM THE READER'S DIGEST, OCTOBER 1950
QUOTED BY PRESIDENT MARION G. ROMNEY
IN THE WELFARE SESSION OF CONFERENCE,
OCTOBER 2, 1976.

A Capsule Course in Human Relations

The five most important words are these:
"I am proud of you."
The four most important words are these:
"What is your opinion?"
The three most important words are these:
"If you please."
The two most important words are these:
"Thank You"
The most important word is this:
"We"
The least important word is this:
"I"

– ROBERT WOODRUFF

Seven Steps in Making a Decision

1. Be clear on the principle involved
2. Take the long look ahead
3. Think objectively
4. Learn from the experience, successes, and failures of others
5. Counsel with others
6. Pray for guidance
7. Decide

Then pray for a confirmation and help to carry your decision through.

– MARION D. HANKS

Beatitudes of a Leader

1. Blessed is the leader who has not sought the high places but who has been drafted into service because of ability and willingness to serve.

2. Blessed is the leader who knows where he is going, why he is going, and how he is going to get there.

3. Blessed is the leader who knows no discouragement, who presents no alibi.

4. Blessed is the leader who seeks for the best for those he serves.

5. Blessed is the leader who leads for the good of the majority, and not for the personal gratification of his personal ideas.

6. Blessed is the leader who develops leaders while leading.

7. Blessed is the leader who marches with the group, and correctly interprets the signs on the pathway that lead to success.

8. Blessed is the leader who has his head in the clouds and his feet on the ground.

9. Blessed is the leader who considers leadership an opportunity to serve.
10. Blessed are LEADERS.

– AUTHOR UNKNOWN

LOVE AND SERVICE

And behold, I tell you these things that ye may
learn wisdom; that ye may learn that when ye are
in the service of your fellow beings ye are only in
the service of your God.

– MOSIAH 2:17

Measuring Our Hearts

There is a passage in The Wizard of Oz that cries out for understanding and, when understood, tells us much of what we need to do. The Tin Man is looking for a heart. In his search, he encounters the Wizard, who teaches him this profound truth: "It is not how much you love, my friend, but by how much you are loved, that a heart is measured."

We are taught to love. Loving God and loving our neighbors are the first two commandments. Part of the Savior's mission was to teach us, by example and by precept, to love.

But just loving is not enough. What the Savior taught over and over—and what the wizard was saying—is that love cannot be passive.

Unless it leads us to service, unless it causes us to reach out, to live the kind of life and be the kind of person who is loved by others, it is not really love; at least it is not Christlike love.

– EXCERPT TAKEN FROM THE CHURCH NEWS,
WRITTEN BY WILLIAM B. SMART

For I Was an Hungered . . .

Then shall the King say unto them on his right hand, Come, ye blessed of my Father, inherit the kingdom prepared for you from the foundation of the world; For I was an hungered, and ye gave me meat; I was thirsty, and ye gave me drink; I was a stranger, and ye took me in: Naked, and ye clothed me. I was sick, and ye visited me; I was in prison, and ye came unto me.

Then shall the righteous answer him, saying Lord, when saw we thee an hungered, and fed thee? Or thirsty, and gave thee drink? When saw we thee a stranger, and took thee in? or naked, and clothed thee? Or when saw we thee sick, or in prison, and came unto thee?

And the king shall answer and say unto them, verily I say unto you, Inasmuch as ye have done it unto one of the least of these my brethren, ye have done it unto me.

– MATTHEW 25:34-40

No Hands but Ours

Shortly after the end of the Second World War, a quaint little French village was bombed by mistake. In the old city square, a large statue of Jesus Christ had stood with his hands outspread in an attitude of invitation. On the pedestal, was the phrase "Come Unto Me."

When the figure was being reassembled, all of the pieces, except for the hands, were found in the rubble. When the hands could not be found, someone suggested that new hands be made.

But the people protested, "No—leave Him without hands!"

So today, in the public square, the restored statue of Christ stands without hands. Now, the words on its base read, "Christ Has No Hands— No Hands But Ours."

– ADAPTED FROM OUR DAILY BREAD

Christ Has No Hands but Our Hands

Christ has no hands but our hands
To do His work today.
He has no feet but our feet
To lead men in his way.
He has no tongue but our tongues
To tell men how He died.
He has no help but our help
To lead men to His side.
What if our hands are busy
With other work than His?
What if our feet are walking
Where sin's allurement is?
What if our tongues are speaking
Of things his lips would spurn?
How can we hope to help Him
Or hasten His return?

– AUTHOR UNKNOWN

Love

Love gives naught but itself and takes from itself.

Love possesses not nor would it be possessed; for love is sufficient unto love.

When you love, you should not say, "God is in my heart," but rather, "I am in the heart of God."

And think not you can direct the course of love—for love, if it finds you worthy, directs your course.

– KAHLIL GIBRAN

Giving is Living

"Go spread, to the Needy, sweet Charity's bread,
For giving is living," the angel said;
"O must I be giving again and again?"
My peevish and willful answer ran.
"Oh, no," said the angel, and her eyes pierced me
through—
"Just give till the Master stops giving to you."

– ANONYMOUS

The Bridge Builder

An old man traveling a long highway,
Came at the evening cold and gray,
To a chasm vast and deep and wide,
The old man crossed in the twilight dim,
The sullen stream held no fears for him;
But he turned when safe on the other side,
And built a bridge to span the tide.
"Old man," cried a fellow pilgrim near,
"You're wasting your time in building here.
Your journey will end with the closing day;
You never again will pass this way.
You have crossed the chasm deep and wide,
Why build you this bridge at even-tide?"
The builder lifted his old gray head;
"Good friend, in the path I have come," he said.
"There followeth after me today
A youth whose feet must pass this way,
This stream that has been as naught to me,
To that fair-haired youth may a pitfall be;

He, too, must cross in the twilight dim—
Good friend, I am building this bridge for him."

– WILLIAM ALLEN DROMGOOLE

Too Hurried to Serve?

In his monthly ward newsletter a young bishop wrote of a group of religion instructors at a theological seminary who were taking a summer course on the life of the Savior—one focusing particularly on the parables.

When final exam time came, the students arrived at the classroom to find a note on the table stating that the exam would be given in another building across campus. The note also said that the test must be finished within a two-hour time period that was starting at that moment.

The students hurried across campus. On the way they passed a little girl crying over a flat tire on her new bike. An old man hobbling painfully toward the library with a cane in one hand, spilled his books on the sidewalk. On a bench, by the union building, sat a shabbily dressed, bearded man with a sign: "I need money to eat. Please help me."

Rushing into the other classroom, the students were met by the professor, who announced that they had all failed the final exam.

The only true test of whether they understood the Savior's life and teaching, he said, was how they treated people in need. Their weeks of study at the feet of a capable professor had taught them a great deal of what Christ had said and done. But nothing they learned in class was as effective as the lesson learned from the professor's exam.

– AUTHOR UNKNOWN

Teach by Showing

Go to the people. Live among them. Learn from them. Serve them. Love them. Plan with them. Start with what they know. Build on what THEY have. Not a piecemeal but an integrated approach. Not relief but release. Mass education through mass participation. Learn by doing. Teach by showing.

– DR. JUAN M. FLAVIER, DOCTOR TO THE BARRIOS

The King's Highway

Once a king had a great highway built for the members of his kingdom. After it was completed, but before it was opened to the public, the king decided to hold a contest. He invited as many as desired to participate. Their challenge was to see who could travel the highway best.

On the day of the contest, the people came. Some of them had fine chariots, some had fine clothing, fine hairdos, or great food. Some young men came in their sports togas and ran along the highway. People traveled the highway all day, but each one, when he arrived at the end, complained to the king that there was a large pile of rocks and debris on the road at one spot, and this had hindered their travel.

At the end of the day, a lone traveler crossed the finish line and wearily walked over to the king. He was tired and dirty—but he addressed the king with great respect, and handed him a bag of gold. He explained, "I stopped along the way to clear away a pile of rocks and debris that was blocking the road. This bag of gold was under it, and I would like you to help me return it to its rightful owner."

The King replied, "You are the rightful owner."

The traveler replied, "Oh no, this is not mine. I've never known so much money."

"Oh yes," said the king, "You've earned this gold, for you have won my contest. He who travels the road best is he who makes the road smoother for those who will follow."

– AUTHOR UNKNOWN

The Return

Instead of allowing yourself to be unhappy, just let your love grow, as God wants it to grow. Seek goodness in others. Love others unselfishly, without thought of return. The return, never fear, will take care of itself.

– HENRY DRUMMOND

The More You Love

The more you love, the more you'll find
That life is good and friends are kind.
For only what we give away
Enriches us from day to day.

– HELEN STEINER RICE

Let Us Serve One Another

A blind man and a lame man happened to come at the same time to a piece of very bad road. The former begged the latter to guide him through his difficulties. "How can I do that," said the lame man, "I am scarcely able to drag myself along? But if you will carry me, I can warn you about obstacles in the way; my eyes will be your eyes and your feet will be mine."

"With all my heart," replied the blind man. "Let us serve one another." So, taking the lame man on his back, they traveled with safety.

– AESOP

The Sun and the Wind

The Wind and the Sun once had a quarrel. The Wind boasted that he was much stronger than the Sun. He said, "I'll show you I'm stronger. See that old man over there with a big coat on? I bet I can make him take his coat off quicker than you can."

"All right," said the Sun, "we'll see." So the Sun went behind a cloud, but left a little hole so he could peep through and see what the Wind did. The Wind blew and blew as hard as he could, causing a terrible storm, but the harder he blew and gusted the tighter the old man wrapped his coat about him. Sometimes it seemed the coat would blow right off, or the old man would topple over. But in the end the poor old Wind had to give up trying, and the sky became calm again.

Then it was the Sun's turn. He came out from behind the cloud and smiled with sunshine at the old man. The sky began to brighten, and birds that had taken cover from the wind came

96

out and chirped sweetly at the old man. After a while, the old man began to smile also, seeing that his big coat was drying after the sudden storm. "What a remarkable day this has become," the old man said, and then he pulled his coat off to enjoy the day.

– AESOP

MISSIONARY WORK

After all that has been said, the greatest and most important duty is to preach the Gospel.

– JOSEPH SMITH JR.

Where Shall I Work Today?

Master, where shall I work today?
My love flowed warm and free.
He pointed out a tiny spot
And said, "Tend that for Me."
I answered quickly—Oh no, not there,
Not any one could see,
No matter how well my work was done;
Not that little spot for me.
When He spoke, He was not stern,
But He answered me tenderly,
"Little one, search that heart of thine;
Are you working for them or for me?
Nazareth was a little place
And so was Galilee."

– MEADE MACGUIRE

Come As You Are

When you were called to work in this [missionary] capacity, you were not required to pass any tests or furnish any proof that you were qualified. No one quizzed you to find out how much you knew about the Gospel, or inquired about your previous experience or training. The only requirement was that you be willing to accept the responsibility of the position you were being asked to fill.

Your Father in Heaven accepted you "as you are" when He called you. He was aware of your weaknesses, your problems, and your knowledge of the Gospel. He knew of your capacity to learn and your potential ability. He knew that with His help, you would be able to fill the position if you sincerely try. You may have weaknesses, lack of knowledge, lack of experience, and problems, but you have our Father in Heaven to help you.

Accept yourself as you are, go about your work with confidence, and seek help from your Father in Heaven through prayer.

– FROM THE MTC SISTERS' MEETING NOTES, 1988.

Upon Leaving Home

I left a quiet harbor
in favor of another, I know not where.
But first, there are seas to cross
And storms to brave.
How could I prefer the foreign deeps
to the encircling arms of my bay?
Because some things
Can only be learned at sea.
Yes, my craft is watertight,
I can navigate the unknown,
And Lo, the winds that fill my sails
Blow from home.

– STEFFANIE RUSSELL

The Emissary

The young man walked down the city street
in a strange land
with his own now far away;
And his newness clashed with the echoing beat
of ox-carts, and small brown feet.
And they say that he preached a better world
to those who loved their own;
And he prayed, "Oh, God, I would my good be
known.
And no one understood. . . .

The young man stepped in the pitted road,
his manner not shiny now,
And gazed on tattered roofs, and backs
beneath their heavy load;
And vaguely sensed the meaning
of eternal days.
And preached, "Come follow me
that you might have rest."
And prayed, "Oh, God, help me to

do my best."
And few men understood. . . .

The young man trudged down
the country lane,
No stranger now,
still searching other paths to roam,
But somehow, unashamed,
a little older now he came.
And deep within his heart he sang,
"This earth is home."
And he preached the brotherhood of man
and peace and charity:
And prayed, "Oh, Lord, that I may be
worthy of such as these,
In some far eternity."
and lo, he understood!

– F. BURTON HOWARD

Called to Serve—in Columbia

A number of years ago, a baby boy was born into a Mormon family in Japan. After a few years, the boy and his family moved to New York City. When he turned his mission papers in, he was certain he would be called to a Japanese Mission to teach his own people, just like his father had done.

However, when the call came, it was to Colombia. Believing there must have been a mistake, he called the mission board and asked them to call President Kimball to find out if there had been some mistake. President Kimball reviewed the call, said there was no mistake, that he was called to go to Colombia.

The young man spent eight long weeks in the MTC trying to learn Spanish. At the end of the eighth week, he contacted President Kimball's office again. "I do not wish to be a bother, but as hard as I try, I cannot learn Spanish. Please send me to Japan." President Kimball said, "Young man, you are to serve in Colombia."

This missionary spent 22 months in Colombia as a junior companion, always following, never saying much, and never really learning the language. Then one day, a few weeks before he was to go home, while he and his companion were waiting for a train, an elderly gentleman tapped him on his shoulder and asked, in broken Spanish, if they were the Mormon missionaries. The old man talked to the missionary and said, in Japanese, that he looked like a person of Japanese decent. The two talked in Japanese for quite a while. After the old man left, the Japanese elder turned to his companion and said they had an appointment at 6:40 that evening and that the older man had given him directions to his house. He had also asked if the elders would talk to some of his family and friends.

Upon arriving at the address, the Japanese gentleman invited them inside where there were 64 Japanese people who couldn't speak any English or Spanish waiting for them. Finally, the elder had the opportunity to teach in Japanese!

How strange, he thought, that he had to come to Colombia to do it. He worked furiously, teaching the group of investigators and helping them understand the Gospel. The missionary baptized all 64 of these people before he finished his mission, including the gentleman from the train station.

The old man had been teaching this group about the gospel out of an old Japanese copy of the Book of Mormon. They had had no one to explain the gospel to them before they met the elders, but they had readily accepted the message because they had been well prepared for it. Before the missionary left Colombia, they asked him to write his testimony in the old Japanese Book of Mormon. After writing his testimony, the missionary turned the page in the well-worn book and read one of the deepest and strongest testimonies he had ever read. Twenty-five years earlier, another missionary had recorded his testimony in this book while serving in Japan. The inspiring words had been penned by the young elder's father.

– AUTHOR UNKNOWN

The Lord, My Companion, and Me

The Lord, my companion and me,
Are a great combination, we three:
For where He would lead us, we go willingly,
The Lord, my companion and me.

The Lord, my companion and me,
Have a work that is endless, you see.
For the good, honest souls must be gathered,
    we're told
By the Lord, my companion and me.

The Lord, my companion and me,
Must pull as a team, constantly,
If we would have power, we will remember each
    hour
It's the Lord first, then my companion, then me.

– LULA ANDERSON

Belief

Every man gives his life for what he believes. Every woman gives her life for what she believes. Sometimes people believe in little or nothing, nevertheless they give up their lives to that little or nothing. One life is all we have, and we live it as we believe. And life without belief is more terrible than dying young.

– ATTRIBUTED TO JOAN OF ARC

Bearers of the Gospel Message

The kind of men we want as bearers of this Gospel message are men who have faith in God; men who have faith in their religion; men who honor their priesthood; men in whom the people who know them have faith and in whom God has confidence—and not some poor unfortunate being who wants to leave. We want men full of the Holy Ghost and the power of God, that they may go forth weeping, bearing precious seed and sowing the seeds of eternal life, and then returning with gladness, bringing their sheaves with them.

Men who bear the words of life among the nations ought to be men of honor, integrity, virtue and purity; and this being the command of God to us, we shall try to carry it out.

– PRESIDENT JOHN TAYLOR

Your Mission is Preparation

Your mission is preparation. It is your school for eternity. You won't forget that, will you? This mission is not just a two-year stretch. This is the time when you cultivate the seeds of godhood so you can help other people on their way toward exaltation. How small are we who think of the mission as just being a stretch of time, some physical things to do, a little studying to do, some praying. This is the most purposeful thing, perhaps, you have ever done in your life and possibly the most purposeful thing some of you will ever do. It's up to you to let this be the prelude to your life, to let it be the beginning of a great and glorious life.

– PRESIDENT SPENCER W. KIMBALL

A Missionary

Sometime between the whirl of teenage activity and the confinement to cane and rocking chair, we find a strange creature called a missionary. Missionaries come in two varieties: elders, and sisters. They come in assorted sizes, weights, and colors—green being the most common among the new ones.

Missionaries are found everywhere, hurrying, climbing, knocking, walking, and getting thrown out. Converts love them, young girls worship them, the law tolerates them, dogs hate them, most people ignore them, and Heaven protects them.

A missionary is a composite. It has the appetite of a horse, the enthusiasm of a firecracker, the patience of Job, the persistence of a Fuller Brush salesman, and the courage of a lion tamer. It likes letters from home, invitations to Sunday dinner, conferences, checks, and visits from the Mission President. It isn't much for tracting in blizzards, ladies who slam doors, hats, suits and dull ties, apartment houses, transfers to hot areas, shaking hands at arm's length with the opposite sex, alarm clocks, and "Dear John" letters.

A missionary is an odd character. It can get homesick, discouraged, and temporarily lose faith in the whole human race. Yet nobody else can knock so boldly with such a shaky hand. Nobody is so early to rise or so tired at 10:30 p.m. And nobody else can get such a thrill at the end of a discouraging day from the words, "Come right in—I've been waiting for you."

A missionary is truth with a pocket full of tracts, and faith with 69 cents in its pocket. "Hey, Dad, where is that check?"

Yes, they are all this, but a strange lump will rise in its throat the day it receives its letter of release, and on arrival home its homecoming speech will probably contain the phrase it once considered trite. "The time I spent in the mission field was the happiest time of my life."

– FROM THE FINNISH MISSION NEWSLETTER, NOVEMBER 1959

The Mission

This is a marvelous plan. It is a process of sanctification. When a missionary is placed in a mission environment of order and discipline where all that is done is in harmony with the Spirit, the missionary experiences a great transformation. The heavens open. Powers are showered out. Mysteries are revealed. Habits are improved. Sanctification begins. Through this process, the missionary becomes a vessel of light that can shine forth the gospel of Jesus Christ in a world in darkness. . . .

Missions are for missionaries. It is a marvelous gift of time, a time given when you can experience glimpses of heavenly life here on earth. It is a time of cleansing and refreshing. It is a special time when the Holy Ghost can seal upon you the knowledge of the great plan for your exaltation. It is one of your best opportunities to become a celestial candidate.

– WILLIAM R. BRADFORD, CONFERENCE REPORT OCT. 1981

The First Epistle of the Elders to the Dead Letter Writers

CHAPTER 1

IN the beginning was the mailbox and the mailbox was void of letters.

2 And the missionaries said, "Let the box be filled," and the box was not filled.

3 And the missionaries beheld the continuing void and were not pleased.

4 And lo, it was the first day of the week and there was no mail delivered, but this was good.

5 But on the second day was the mail delivered; yet the box remained empty.

6 Yea, even from the second day unto the seventh was the mail delivered.

7 Even so, the box retained its void.

8 And yea, great mists of darkness spread forth from the void and enshrouded the missionaries. Yea, and did bring much sadness to their otherwise cheery days.

9 Even the long hours of fruitless tracting, being attacked by the fowls of the air, and being pursued by the beasts of the field were not as disheartening as the lack of blessed objects known as letters.

10 Yet they persisted.

CHAPTER 2

AND, Lo, on the second day of the second week the mists still encircled the mailbox.

2 And on the third day, from within the depths of the void was a single postcard.

3 And this postcard put forth a ray of light that pierced the darkness and overcame the mists.

4 And the missionaries were well pleased, and there was much rejoicing.

5 But, alas, their exclamations of joy were in vain. For the postcard was for someone else.

6 But if their joy was so exceedingly great over someone else's mail, how great would be their joy at partaking of their own mail?

CHAPTER 3

BUT some will say, A letter. A letter. We have already written a letter. We have no need to write any more letters.

2 Know ye not that there are more days than one, and more events than one in a day? Why think ye that these events need not be reported?

3 Yea, and ye need not worry that your letters will go unanswered.

4 But you should say, I will go and write the letter that a missionary requests. For I know that he giveth no requests except he be prepared to speedily respond.

5 And we give unto you the parable of the self-addressed envelopes.

6 When the missionary departed into the far off land he gave a certain number of self-addressed stamped envelopes to his friends.

7 Unto one he gave five, unto another he gave two, and unto the third he gave one.

8 And while he was gone, he that was given the five envelopes wrote five letters, then in his zeal wrote five letters more.

9 The same with him that had two envelopes; He wrote two letters and then two letters more.

10 But he that was given the one self-addressed envelope became slothful and careless.

And he lost the envelope, even that which he was given.

11 And when the missionary came home he went unto his friends. And he that had written ten letters was warmly greeted.

12 The same with him that had written four letters.

13 But he that had written none at all was given nothing more than a fishy, wimp-like handshake.

CHAPTER 4

AND the missionary said unto his friend; lovest thou me?

2 And the friend said, of course I love thee. Then the missionary said, fill my mailbox.

3 He saith a second time, friend, lovest thou me? And the friend said, thou knowest that I love thee. He then said, fill my mailbox.

4 He then spake a third time saying, lovest thou me? And the friend said, thou knowest all things, thou knowest that I love thee.

5 Then the missionary said, stuff my mailbox.

6 And the vision is become unto all as the words of a letter that is sealed in the envelope that men deliver to one who is not serving a mission saying,

Read this, I pray thee; and he saith, I cannot, for it is not mine.

7 And the letter is delivered to him that is serving a mission saying, read this I pray thee; and he saith, why sure.

8 Therefore you should proceed to do a marvelous work for a missionary, even a marvelous work and a wonder by writing a letter.

– THE MISSIONARIES OF THE TEXAS SAN ANTONIO MISSION

Live Your Religion

One good man—one man who does not put on his religion once a week with his Sunday coat, but wears it for his working dress, and lets the thought of God grow in him, and through him, until everything he says and does becomes religious—that man is worth a thousand sermons. He is a living Gospel—he is the image of God. And men see his good works, and admire them in spite of themselves, and see that they are Godlike, and that God's grace is no dream, but that the Holy Spirit is still among men. They get a glimpse of God, and glorify their Father who is in heaven.

– CHARLES KINGSLEY

The Standard of Truth

Our missionaries are going forth in different nations. The standard of truth has been erected; no unhallowed hand can stop the work from progressing. Persecutions may rage, mobs may combine, armies may assemble, calumny may defame; but the truth of God will go forth boldly, nobly and independent, till it has penetrated every continent, visited every clime, swept every country and sounded in every ear, till the purposes of God shall be accomplished, and the Great Jehovah shall say the work is done.

– JOSEPH SMITH, EXCERPT FROM THE WENTWORTH LETTER

The Convert

These were the results of a questionnaire given to
three thousand recent converts:

1. How did you first hear the gospel?

   Missionary   45%

   Neighbor   15%

   Kin   40 %

2. What phase of the gospel attracted you to it?

   Teachings about God   35%

   The Book of Mormon   26 %

   The Plan of Salvation   39%

3. If missionaries first brought the gospel, what
   impressed you most about them?

   Their apparent conviction   70%

   Their knowledge of the Bible 30%

4. Which do you feel helped you most to conversion?

   Cottage meetings   25%

   Branch meetings with Saints   10%

   Personal talks with missionaries and others

                                 65%

5. When did you sense that the restored gospel was true?

Right at first	65%
After all the lessons	35%

– ORIGINAL SOURCE UNKNOWN

A Christ-Centered Mission

If you go on a mission to preach the Gospel with lightness and frivolity in your hearts, looking for this and that, and to learn what is in the world, and not having your minds riveted—yes, I may say riveted—on the cross of Christ, you will go and return in vain. Go forth weeping, bearing precious seed, full of the power of God, and full of faith to heal the sick even by the touch of your hand, rebuking and casting out foul spirits, and causing the poor among men to rejoice, and you will return bringing your sheaves with you. Let your minds be centered on your missions and labor earnestly to bring souls to Christ.

– BRIGHAM YOUNG

OBEDIENCE

If ye love me, keep my commandments.

– JOHN14: 15

The Kite is Held Up by the String

While flying a kite, I once asked my father, "Dad, what holds the kite up?"

"The string," he replied.

"No, Dad, the string holds it down, not up."

"If you think so, let go of the string," he said, "and see what happens."

I let go—and the kite began to fall! It seems odd that the very thing that seems to keep the kite down is actually what keeps it up. And this is true not only of kites but of life. Those strings that are tied to us, those rules and regulations that seem to hold us down, are actually holding us up.

And certainly in the realm of the spirit, in the field of faith, this same truth holds with even greater force. The word "religion" is said to come from a Latin root meaning "to hold back" or tie back. And this is what religion does. It provides the string to the soaring kite of our spirit; it keeps us from falling! It binds us to great values; it attaches us to great causes; it helps us fly high in the aid of God's truth and lifts us until our heads touch the stars and our lives take on the beauty of men and women who are bound closely to God. . . .

Men and women who turn their lives over to God will find out that He can make a lot more out of their lives than they can. He will deepen their joys, expand their vision, quicken their minds, strengthen their muscles, lift their spirits, multiply their blessings, increase their opportunities, comfort their souls, raise up friends, and pour out peace. Whoever will lose his life to God will find he has Eternal Life.

– EZRA TAFT BENSON, MAY 1975

Battle Orders

Some years ago, during the Korean War, an army leader tried to act self-sufficient. As a platoon leader he received an order from his commanding General that read, "I am sending you and your men to a ridge located at the following map points. You are to arrive at the ridge at precisely 0200 hours and observe the enemy until 0210 hours." That meant he'd have to just sit for ten minutes, looking at the enemy from this secret place high above them. He was directed to leave the ridge at exactly ten minutes after two.

He took his men to the ridge as told. He arrived on schedule at 0200 hours. He saw the enemy directly below, sound asleep, tanks dismounted, guns not even assembled. He thought, "If we wait for ten minutes one of my men may make a sound, and the enemy could be alerted to full strength." So, thinking the General had made an error, he sent his men down the hill to engage the enemy. When they reached the bottom at precisely 0202 hours, the air was filled with artillery shells from the allied guns many miles away—an all out attack.

Everyone died but the platoon leader. At 0210 hours the shelling stopped. At 0211 amid the stony silence, the platoon leader said but one thing; "I didn't know what the General knew."

– AS TOLD BY SGT. STEVE SEIDEMAN,
UIJONGBU, KOREA, DEC., 1995

Arabian Horses

It has been said that horses in Arabia go through a rigorous selection process. To live in this hot, desert climate, one depends on the unfailing obedience and loyalty of his horse. The horses are tested in order to select the very best. For one of the tests, the horses are worked hard for three days with no food and very little water. At the end of the three days they are placed next to a corral where there are troughs of clear water and hay. The horses, thirsty and fatigued, see the food and water and strain against the gates. When the gate is opened, the horses gallop towards the troughs. Just as the first horse reaches the trough, a whistle is sounded for the horses to return. The horses that take a quick drink before returning to their masters are eliminated. The horses that are chosen are those that without hesitancy obey their master's command and return.

– JOHN J. HURST

The Man in the Glass

When you get what you want in your struggle for
    self
And the world makes you king for a day,
Just go to the mirror and look at yourself
And see what that man has to say.

For it isn't your father, your mother, or wife
Whose judgment upon you must pass;
The fellow whose verdict counts most in your life
Is the one staring back from the glass.

Some people may think you a straight-shootin' chum
And think you're a wonderful guy;
But the man in the glass says your only a bum
If you can't look him straight in the eye.

He's the fellow to please, never mind all the rest;
For he's with you clear to the end.
And you've passed your most dangerous, difficult test
If the man in the glass is your friend.

You may fool the whole world down the pathway
    of years
And get pats on the back as you pass;
But your final reward will be heartaches and tears
If you've cheated the man in the glass.

– DALE WIMBROW

The Forty Wrestlers

Long ago in the days when the ruling passion of the Roman emperor, Nero, was the extermination of the Christians, he had a band of soldiers known as "The Emperor's Wrestlers." They were picked from the best and the bravest of the land and recruited from the great athletes of the Roman amphitheater. When going into battle they would chant: "We, the wrestlers, wrestling for thee, O emperor, to win for thee the victory and from thee, the victor's crown."

When the Roman army was sent to fight in far away Gaul, no soldiers were braver or more loyal than this band of wrestlers led by their centurion, Vespasian. But news reached Nero that the Christian faith had come among the wrestlers and many had accepted it.

To be a Christian meant death, even to those who served Nero best. So a decree was dispatched to Vespasian, "If there be any among the soldiers who cling to the faith of the Christians, they must die!"

The decree was received in the dead of winter, while the soldiers were camped on the shore of a frozen lake. The winter had been hard, but the hardships the men had endured together had only served to unite them more closely. So it was with a sinking heart that Vespasian read the emperor's message. He called the soldiers together and asked, "Are there any among you who cling to the faith of the Christians? If so let him step forward!" Forty wrestlers instantly stepped forward two paces, respectfully saluted, and stood at attention. Vespasian paused. He had not expected so many. "The decree has come from your emperor," he said, "that any who cling to the faith of the Christians must die! For the sake of your country, your comrades, your loved ones, renounce this false faith!" Not one of the forty moved. "Until sundown I shall await your answer," said Vespasian. Sundown came. Again the question was asked, "Are there any among you who cling to the faith of the Christians? If so let them step forward!"

Again the forty wrestlers stepped forward and stood at attention. Vespasian pleaded with them long and earnestly without prevailing upon a single man to deny his Lord. Finally he said, "The decree of the Emperor must be obeyed, but I am not willing that your blood be on your comrades.

I am going to order you to march out on the lake of ice and I shall leave you there to the mercy of the elements. Fires, however, will be burning on the shore, and at the largest I will be waiting to welcome any willing to renounce this false faith."

The forty wrestlers were stripped and then without a word they wheeled, and falling into columns of four, marched out toward the lake of ice. As they marched, they broke into a chorus with the old chant of battle, "Forty wrestlers, wrestling for thee, O Christ, to win for thee the victory and from thee, the victor's crown!"

All through the long hours of the night Vespasian stood by his campfire and waited, and all through the long night came back to him fainter and fainter the wrestlers' song. As it neared morning one figure, overcome by exposure, crept quietly toward the fire. In the extremity of his suffering he renounced his Lord. Faintly, but clearly, from out of the darkness came the song.

"Thirty-nine wrestlers, wrestling for thee, O Christ, to win for thee the victory and from thee, the victor's crown!"

Vespasian looked at the figure drawing close to the fire and then out into the darkness whence came the song of faith. Once again he looked. Perhaps he saw the greater light shining there in the darkness! Off came his helmet, down went his shield and he sprang upon the ice crying, "Forty wrestlers, wrestling for thee, O Christ, to win for thee the victory and from thee, the victor's crown!"

– AUTHOR UNKNOWN

Your Conscience

There's an odd little voice
Always speaking within
And it prompts you to duty
And it warns you from sin
And what is most strange
It makes itself heard
Though it gives not a sound
And says never a word.
You follow it.

– ELDER PAUL H. DUNN

On the Titanic

When the ill-fated 'Titanic' steamed majestically through the darkness on her maiden voyage to New York, on 14th April 1912, there were more than two thousand people enjoying the liner's comforts. The *Washington Post* recalls one of the tragic incidents of that night:

In the wheel room, a uniformed officer hummed at his task as he directed the destinies of an ocean greyhound that was setting a speed record. The phone rang. A minute passed! Another minute! The officer was busy! The third precious minute passed. The officer, his trivial task completed, stepped to the phone. From the crow's nest—"Iceberg dead ahead! Reverse engines!" But as he rushed to the controls, the "pride of the seas" crashed into the iceberg amid a deafening roar. Three precious minutes! Attention to trivial details and sixteen hundred people paid with their lives.

– ANTHONY P. CASTLE

Return with Honor

As a young man, I had an opportunity to serve in the U.S. Air Force as a jet-fighter pilot. Each unit in our squadron had a motto that would inspire its efforts. Our unit motto—displayed on the side of our aircraft—was "Return with Honor." This motto was a constant reminder to us of our determination to return to our home base with honor only after having expended all of our efforts to successfully complete every aspect of our mission.

This same motto, "Return with Honor," can be applied to each of us in our eternal plan of progression. Having lived with our Heavenly Father and having come to earth, we must have determination to return with honor to our heavenly home. Just as aircraft pilots must obey certain rules in order to avoid disaster, there are laws, ordinances, and covenants we must understand and obey as we go through this earthly life if we are to reach our goal of eternal life.

During pilot training, we spent hours in a device that simulated real flight. There, an instructor would teach us about emergencies that could occur when flying a jet fighter at the speed of sound. For each emergency, we were taught how to avoid disaster. We would practice each procedure over and over so that when a real emergency came we would have developed what was called an automatic, or conditioned, response. We would know exactly what to do if the fire-warning light lit up or the panel indicated some technical failure in the airplane. This training process can be compared to the lessons we learn in our homes and in our church meetings. . . .

As a father, I put my arms around each of my boys as they left to serve their missions and whispered in their ear, "Return with honor." I can picture our Father in Heaven putting his arms around each of us as we left his presence and whispering the same thing, "Return with honor."

– BISHOP ROBERT D. HALES,
GENERAL CONFERENCE ADDRESS, APRIL 1990

The Lark

Sin like a journey begins with the first step, and wisdom and experience teach that it is easier to resist the first temptation than later ones when a pattern of transgression has begun to develop. This is demonstrated in the story of the lark.

Sitting in the high branches of a tree, safe from harm, he saw a traveler walking through the forest carrying a mysterious small black box. The lark flew down and perched on the traveler's shoulder.

"What do you have in the little black box?" He asked.

"Worms" the traveler replied.

"Are they for sale?"

"Yes, and very cheaply," he said. "The price is only one feather per worm."

The lark thought for a moment. I must have a million feathers; surely I won't miss one of them. Here is an opportunity to get a good dinner for no work at all. So he told the man he'd buy one.

He searched carefully under his wing for a tiny feather. He winced a bit as he pulled it out but the size and quality of the worm made him quickly forget the pain. High up in the tree he began to sing as beautifully as before.

The next day he saw the man and once again exchanged a feather for a worm. What an effortless way to get dinner. Each day the lark surrendered a feather and each loss seemed to hurt less and less. In the beginning he had many feathers but as the days passed he found it more difficult to fly. Finally, after the loss of one of his primary feathers, he could no longer reach the top of the tree, let alone fly up into the sky. In fact he could do no more than flutter a few feet in the air, and was forced to seek his food with the bickering sparrows.

The man with the worms came no more because there were no more feathers to pay for the meals and the lark no longer sang because he was ashamed of his fallen state.

– AN EXCERPT FROM SPENCER W. KIMBALL'S BOOK,
THE MIRACLE OF FORGIVENESS

OUR SAVIOR
JESUS CHRIST

For God so loved the world, that He gave his Only Begotten Son, that whosoever believeth in him should not perish, but have everlasting life.

– JOHN 3:16

The Son

This evening, very briefly, I sat in silent solitude

And watched with fascinated awe the setting of the sun.

I saw first its quiet beauty, and I knew that it had shone

So that I, and others with me, might see all that beauty is.

For a moment then I closed my eyes and felt with pleasured peace

The warming of the sun's last rays, its gift, with light, to me.

Pausing suddenly I listened as my mind began to stir—

Telling me of things not known about the sun and me.

I thought of my dependence, the light I use, and warmth;

And how my world is set on course, revolving without my choice.

And then I made that quantum leap—to see, to feel, to know

144

That what I truly saw tonight was not the source
   itself—

But was, as I, responding—commanded and
   complying,

Fulfilling now its destiny, a constant, ever giving.

I wondered, as the darkness spread, of the true
   source I had not seen.

The Son my mind saw clearly now, and what He
   did for me:

The Garden and the drops of blood, the cross on
   which He hung,

The price He paid to light my life, the suffering
   that He bore.

And now his warmth and shining glow, much
   more than the sun above,

Radiated out so powerfully with wondrous light
   and love,

To set on course my own small life, with purpose
   to go forth,

And share with constancy and love—His light
   with everyone.

– BRENTON G. YORGASON

If Jesus Came to Your House

If Jesus came to your house to spend a day or two
If He came unexpectedly, I wonder what you'd do.
Oh, I know you'd give your nicest to such an
   honored guest
And all the food you'd serve to Him would be
   your very best.
And you'd keep assuring Him you're glad to have
   Him there
That serving Him in your own home is joy
   beyond compare.

But when you saw Him coming would you meet
   Him at the door?
With your arms outstretched in welcome to your
   Heavenly Visitor?
Or would you have to change your clothes before
   you let Him in?
Or hide some magazines and put the Bible where
   they'd been?

Would you turn off the radio and hope He hadn't
    heard
And wish you hadn't uttered the last loud hasty word?
Would you hide your worldly music and put some
    hymnbooks out?
Could you let Jesus just walk right in, or would
    you rush about?

And I wonder if the Savior spent a day or two
    with you
Would you go right on doing the things you
    always do?
Would you keep right on saying the things you
    always say?
Would life for you continue as it does from day
    to day?
Would your family conversation keep up it's
    usual pace
Or would you find it hard each meal to say the
    table grace?
Would you sing the songs you always sing and
    read the books you read

And let Him know the things on which your
mind and spirit feed?

Would you take Jesus with you every place you
planned to go?
Or would you maybe change your plans for just a
day or so?
Would you be glad to have Him meet your very
closest friends?
Or would you hope they'd stay away, until His
visit ends?

Would you be glad to have Him stay forever on
and on?
Or would you sigh with great relief, when He at
last was gone?
It might be interesting to know the things that
you would do
If Jesus Christ in person, came to spend some
time with you.

– AUTHOR UNKNOWN

The Birdcage

There once was a man named George Thomas, a pastor in a small New England town. One Easter Sunday morning he came to church carrying a rusty, bent old bird cage, and set it on the pulpit. Several eyebrows were raised, and Pastor Thomas began to speak.

"I was walking through town yesterday when I saw a young boy coming towards me, swinging this bird cage. On the bottom of the cage were three little wild birds, shivering with cold and fright. I stopped the lad and asked, 'What have you got there, son?'"

"Just some old birds," came the reply.

"What are you going to do with them?" I asked.

"Pull out their feathers to make 'em fight. I'm gonna have a real good time."

"But you'll get tired of these birds sooner or later—what will you do then?"

"Oh, I got some cats—they like birds. I'll give 'em to them."

The pastor was silent a moment.

"How much do you want for those birds, son?"

"Huh? Why, you don't want these birds, mister. They're just plain old dumb field birds. They don't sing—and they ain't even pretty!"

"How much?"

The boy sized up the pastor as if he were crazy, and said, "Ten dollars?"

The Pastor reached in his pocket and took out a ten-dollar bill. He placed it in the boy's hand. In a flash, the boy was gone. The pastor picked up the cage and gently carried it to the end of the alley, where there was a tree and a grassy spot. Setting the cage down he opened the door, and by softly tapping the bars he persuaded the birds out, setting them free.

Then the pastor began to tell the second part of his story.

One day Satan and Jesus were having a conversation. Satan had just come from the Garden of Eden, and he was gloating and boasting. "Yes sir, I just caught a world full of people down there. Set me a trap, used bait I knew they couldn't resist. Got 'em all!"

"What are you going to do with them?" Jesus asked.

"Oh, I'm gonna have fun! I'm gonna teach them how to marry and divorce each other, how to hate and abuse each other, how to invent guns and bombs and kill each other. I'm really gonna have fun!"

"And what will you do with them when you grow tired of that?"

"Oh, kill 'em. Damn 'em."

"How much for these people?" Jesus asked.

"Oh, you don't want these people. They ain't no good. Why, you take them, and they'll just hate you. They'll spit on you, and curse you, and kill you—you of all wouldn't want these people!"

"How much?"

Satan looked at Jesus and answered, "All your tears and blood."

Jesus paid the price, picked up the cage, and opened the door.

– AUTHOR UNKNOWN

Two Hands

While walking in the sand one day
I tripped and fell and while I lay
Two hands reached out to lift me high,
One hand moist, the other hand dry.
One hand was tattered, worn, and abused.
The other hand soft, smooth and unused.
I knew not which hand to take in mine
To lift me up and guide me through time.
For one hand would lead me back home to God,
The other away from the iron rod.
Cautiously I picked the tattered, torn hand
It lifted me up and again I could stand.
I knew then I'd picked the Lord's helping hand,
For Satan would've left me there in the sand.
I wondered why His hand was so worn and abused
And then I remembered how much it was used.

– KARA BISHOP

The Interview

A man passed away, was resurrected, and was waiting in a room to be interviewed. Another man was ahead of him. The door opened, the first man entered, and the door closed. The man on the outside could hear the conversation on the other side of the door. The interviewer began: "I would like you to tell me what you think of Jesus Christ."

"Well, He was born of a virgin in Bethlehem. He lived 33 years or so, spending the last three in His ministry organizing His Church, choosing His apostles to direct it, giving the Gospel to direct our lives."

The interviewer stopped him and said, "Yes, that's all true, but I want you to tell me what *you* think of Christ."

"Well, He was tortured and crucified that we might have eternal life. Three days later He was resurrected that we might return to our Heavenly Father."

"Yes, that is true, but tell me what *you* think of Jesus Christ."

The man paused, a little perplexed now, and then continued: "Well, He restored the gospel in its fullness to the earth through Joseph Smith. He reorganized His church, gave us temples wherein we might do work to redeem our dead. He gave us family prayer and family home evening where we might unite with our families. He gave us the priesthood to heal the sick and personal ordinances for our salvation and exaltation."

The interviewer again stopped him and said, "Thank you. All of what you have said to me is true." The man was then invited to leave the room. After he left, the door opened and the second man entered. As he approached the interviewer, his eyes opened wide. He fell upon his knees and cried, "My Lord, My God."

– AUTHOR UNKNOWN

Jesus Christ

Here is a man who was born in an obscure village, the child of a peasant woman. He grew up in another obscure village. He worked in a carpenter shop until he was 30, and then for years he was an itinerant preacher. He never wrote a book. He never held any office. He never went to college. He never put his foot inside a big city. He never traveled more than 200 miles from the place of his birth. He never did any of the things that accompany greatness. He had no credentials but himself. He had nothing to do with this world except the naked power of his divine manhood.

While still a young man, the tide of popular opinion turned against him. His friends ran away. One of them denied him; another betrayed him. He was turned over to his enemies. He went through the mockery of a trial. He was nailed on the cross between two thieves. His executors gambled for the one piece of property he had on earth, his coat. When he was dead, he was taken down and laid in a borrowed grave through the pity of a friend.

Nineteen centuries have come and gone, and today he is the center of the human race. All the armies of the world that ever marched, and that ever were built, and all the navies that were ever built, and all the parliaments that ever sat, and all the kings that ever reigned, put together, have not affected the life of man upon this earth as did that one solitary life.

— BRUCE BARTON

The Purpose in Gethsemane

All those who journey soon or late,
Must pass within the garden's gate;
Must kneel alone in darkness there,
And battle with some fierce despair.
God pity those who cannot say:
'Not mine but thine;' who only pray,
'Let this cup pass,' and cannot see
The purpose in Gethsemane.

– ELLA WHEELER WILCOX

By the Waters Of Galilee

Behold a teacher went forth to teach
Some two thousand years ago;
Before the age of the telegraph,
The car or the radio.
He had no books and no magazines,
And held no scholastic degree,
But men still ponder the things he taught
By the waters of Galilee.

He didn't teach that the world was round,
That water was H_2O;
The fourth dimension has lost it's kick,
There's little we do not know.
But it's not the mechanics this old world needs;
But rather, to make men free;
More teachers to teach as the Master taught
By the waters of Galilee.

– AUTHOR UNKNOWN

The Touch of the Master's Hand

'Twas battered and scarred, and the auctioneer
Thought it scarcely worth his while
To waste much time on the old violin,
But he held it up with a smile.

"What am I bid, good friends?" he cried.
"Who'll start the bidding for me?
One dollar! Only one? And who'll make it two?
Two dollars, once. And three!

Three dollars, once; And three dollars, twice;
And going for three." But no,
From the room, far back, a gray-haired man
Came forward and picked up the bow.

Then, wiping the dust from the old violin,
And tightening the loose strings,
He played a melody pure and sweet
As a caroling angel sings.

The music ceased, and the auctioneer
With a voice that was quiet and low,
Said, "What am I bid for the old violin?"
And he held it up with the bow.

"One thousand dollars, and who'll make it two?
Two thousand dollars, and three!
Three thousand, once. And three thousand, twice.
And going, and gone," said he.

The people cheered, but some of them cried,
"We do not quite understand
What changed its worth?" Swift came the reply.
"Twas the touch of the Master's hand."

And many a man with life out of tune
And battered and scarred with sin,
Is auctioned cheap to the thoughtless crowd
Much like this old violin.

A mess of pottage, a glass of wine.
A game—and he travels on.
He is "going" once, and "going" twice.
And "going," and almost "gone."

But the Master comes, and the thoughtless crowd
Never can quite understand
The worth of a soul and the change that is wrought,
By the touch of the Master's hand.

– MYRA BROOKS WELCH

The Light of the World

"The Light of the World" is the title of a famous picture by Holman Hunt painted in 1854. It portrays Christ, thorn-crowned, and carrying a lantern, knocking at a closed door. When the artist showed the completed picture to some friends, one pointed out what seemed to be an omission. "You have put no handle on the door," he said to Mr. Hunt. The artist replied, "We must open to the Light—the handle is on the inside."

– ANTHONY P. CASTLE

The File Room

In that place between wakefulness and dreams, I found myself in the room. There were no distinguishing features except for the one wall covered with small index-card files. They were like the ones in libraries that list titles by author or subject in alphabetical order. But these files, which stretched from floor to ceiling and seemed endless in either direction, had very different headings. As I drew near the wall of files, the first to catch my attention was one that read "Girls I Have Liked." I opened it and began flipping through the cards. I quickly shut it, shocked to realize that I recognized the names written on each one. And then without being told, I knew exactly where I was. This lifeless room with its small files was a catalog system for my life. Here were written the actions of my every moment, big and small, in a detail my memory couldn't match.

A sense of wonder and curiosity, coupled with horror, stirred within me as I began randomly opening files. Some brought joy and sweet memories; others a sense of shame and regret so intense that I would look over my shoulder to see if anyone were watching. A file named "Friends" was next to one marked "Friends I Have Betrayed."

The titles ranged from the mundane to the outright weird. "Books I Have Read," "Lies I Have Told," "Comfort I Have Given," "Jokes I Have Laughed At." Some were almost hilarious in their exactness: "Things I've Yelled at My Brothers." Others I couldn't laugh at: "Things I Have Done in Anger," "Things I Have Muttered Under My Breath at My Parents." I never ceased to be surprised by the contents. Often there were many more cards than I expected. Sometimes fewer than I hoped.

The sheer volume of the life I had lived overwhelmed me. Could it be possible that I had the time in my 20 years to write each of these thousands or even millions of cards? But each card confirmed this truth. Each was written in my own handwriting. Each signed with my signature.

When I pulled out the file marked "Songs I Have Listened To," I realized the files grew to contain their contents. The cards were packed tightly, and yet after two or three yards, I hadn't found the end of the file. I shut it, ashamed, not so much by the quality of music, but more by the vast amount of time I knew that file represented.

When I came to a file marked "Lustful Thoughts," I felt a chill run through my body. I pulled the file out only an inch, not willing to test its size, and drew out a card. I shuddered at its detailed content. I felt sick to think that such a moment had been recorded. An almost animal rage broke over me. One thought dominated my mind: "No one must ever see these cards! No one must ever see this room!"

"I have to destroy them!" In an insane frenzy I yanked the file out. Its size didn't matter now. I had to empty it and burn the cards. But as I took it at one end and began pounding it on the floor, I could not dislodge a single card. I became desperate and pulled out a card, only to find it as strong as steel when I tried to tear it.

Defeated and utterly helpless, I returned the file to its slot. Leaning my forehead against the wall, I let out a long, self-pitying sigh. And then I saw it. The title bore "People I Have Shared the Gospel With." The handle was brighter than those around it, newer, almost unused. I pulled on its handle and a small box not more than three inches long fell into my hands. I could count the cards it contained on one hand.

And then the tears came. I began to weep. Sobs so deep that the hurt started in my stomach and shook through me. I fell on my knees and cried. I cried out of shame, from the overwhelming shame of it all. The rows of file shelves swirled in my tear filled eyes. No one must ever, ever know of this room. I must lock it up and hide the key.

But then as I pushed away the tears, I saw Him.

No, please not Him. Not here. Oh, anyone but Jesus. I watched helplessly as He began to open the files and read the cards. I couldn't bear to watch His response. And in the moments I could bring myself to look at His face, I saw a sorrow deeper than my own. He seemed to intuitively go to the worst boxes. Why did He have to read every one?

Finally, He turned and looked at me from across the room. He looked at me with pity in His eyes. But this was a pity that didn't anger me. I dropped my head, covered my face with my hands and began to cry again. He walked over and put His arm around me. He could have said so many things. But He didn't say a word. He just cried with me. Then He got up and walked back to the wall of files. Starting at one end of the room, He took out a file and, one by one, began to sign His name over mine on each card.

"No!" I shouted rushing to Him. All I could find to say was "No, no," as I pulled the card from Him. His name shouldn't be on these cards. But there it was, written in red so rich, so dark, and so alive. The name of Jesus covered mine. It was written in His blood.

He gently took the card back. He smiled a sad smile and began to sign the cards. I don't think

I'll ever understand how He did it so quickly, but the next instant it seemed I heard Him close the last file and walk back to my side. He placed His hand on my shoulder and said, "It is finished." I stood up, and He led me out of the room. There was no lock on its door. There were still cards to be written.

– AUTHOR UNKNOWN

OVERCOMING OBSTACLES

The harder the conflict,
the more glorious the triumph.
What we obtain too cheaply
we esteem too lightly.

– THOMAS PAINE

Footprints

One night a man had a dream. He dreamed he was walking along the beach with the Lord. Across the sky flashed scenes from his life.

When the last scene of his life flashed before him, he looked back at the footprints in the sand. He noticed that at times of his life there was only one set of footprints. He also noticed that these were the lowest and saddest times in his life.

This bothered him, and he asked the Lord, "You said that once I decided to follow You, You'd walk with me all the way. But during the most troublesome times in my life, there is only one set of footprints. Why, when I needed You most, did You leave me?" The Lord replied, "My son, I love you and would never leave you. During those times of trial and suffering, when you see only one set of footprints, it was then that I was carrying you."

– ANONYMOUS

What God Hath Promised

God hath not promised skies always blue,
Flower-strewn pathways all our lives through.
God hath not promised sun without rain,
Joy without sorrow, peace without pain.
God hath not promised we shall not know
Toil and temptation, trouble and woe.
He hath not told us we shall not bear
Many a burden, many a care.
But God hath promised strength for the day,
Rest for the laborer, light for the way.
Grace for the trials, help from above,
Unfailing sympathy, undying love.

– ANNE JOHNSON FLINT

Brave

God, make me brave for this life: Oh, braver than
   this.
Let me straighten after pain, as a tree straightens
   after the rain,
Shining and lovely again.
God, make me brave for life: Much braver than this.
As the blown grass lifts, let me rise
from the sorrow with quiet eyes,
knowing thy way is wise.
God, make me brave; life brings
such blinding things.
Help me to keep my sight:
Help me to see alright
that out of dark comes light.

– AUTHOR UNKNOWN

Cattle

I like the story and the philosophy of storms expressed by a rugged old-time cowboy who said he had learned life's most important lesson from Hereford cows. All his life he had worked cattle ranches where winter storms took a heavy toll among the herds. Freezing rains whipped across the prairies. Howling, bitter winds piled snow into enormous drifts. Temperatures dropped quickly to below-zero degrees. Flying ice cut into the flesh. In this maelstrom of nature's violence, most cattle would turn their backs to the icy blasts and slowly drift downwind, mile upon mile. Finally, intercepted by a boundary fence, they would pile up against the barrier and die by the scores.

But Hereford cows acted differently. They would head into the wind and stand shoulder-to-shoulder facing the storm's blast. "You most always found the Herefords alive and well," said the cowboy. "I guess that is the greatest lesson I ever learned on the prairies—just face life's storms."

NORMAN VINCENT PEALE

The Road Is Rough

The road is rough, I said.
Dear Lord, there are stones that hurt me so,
And He said, dear child, I understand,
I walked it long ago,
But there's a cold green path, I said,
Let me walk there for a time.
No child, He gently answered me,
That green road does not climb.
My burden, I said, is far too great;
How can I bear it so?
My child, He said, I remember its weight.
I carried my cross, you know.
I wish I had friends with me,
Who would make my way their own.
Ah, yes... He said, Gethsemane
Was hard to face alone.
And so I walked the stony path,
Content at last to know,
That where my Master hath not gone,
I would not have to go.

Strangely then I did find friends,
My burdens grew less sore.
For I remembered long ago,
He walked the way before.

– LEONA B. GATES

Good Timber

The tree that never had to fight
For sun and sky and air and light,
That stood out in the open plains
And always got its share of rain,
Never became a forest king,
But lived and died a scrubby thing.

The man who never had to toil
To heaven from the common soil,
Who never had to win his share
Of sun and sky and light and air,
Never became a manly man,
But lived and died as he began.

Good timber does not grow in ease
The stronger the wind the tougher the trees;
The farther sky, and the greater length;
The more the storm, and the more the strength;
By sun and cold, by rain and snows,
In tree or man good timber grows.

Where thickest stands the forest growth
We find the patriarchs of both:
And they hold converse with the stars
Whose broken branches show the scars
Of many winds and much strife—
This is the common law of life.

– DOUGLAS MALLOCK

Don't Quit

When things go wrong, as they sometimes will
When the road you're trudging seems all up hill;
When the funds are low and the debts are high
And you want to smile, but you have to sigh;
When care is pressing down a bit
Rest if you must, but don't you quit.

Life is strange with its twists and turns
As everyone of us sometimes learns;
And many a fellow turns about
When he might have won had he stuck it out;
Don't give up though the pace seems slow—
You may succeed with another blow.

Often the goal is nearer than
It seems to a faint and faltering man;
Often the struggler has given up
When he might have captured the victor's cup;
And he learned too late when the night came down
How close he was to the golden crown.

Success is failure turned inside out—
The silver tint of the clouds of doubt,
And you never can tell how close you are,
It may be near when it seems afar.
So stick to the fight when you're hardest hit,
It's when things seem worst that you mustn't quit.

– AUTHOR UNKNOWN

The Blacksmith

You perhaps recall the story of the blacksmith who gave his heart to God. Though conscientious in his living, still he was not prospering materially. In fact, it seemed that from the time of his conversion he had more trouble, affliction and loss than ever before. Everything seemed to be going wrong.

One day a friend who was not a Christian, stopped at the blacksmith's little forge to talk to him. Sympathizing with him in some of his trials, the friend said, "It seems strange to me that so much affliction should pass over you, just at the time when you have become an earnest Christian. Of course I don't want to weaken your faith in God, or anything like that. But here you are with God's help and guidance, and yet things seem to be getting steadily worse. I can't help wondering why it is."

The blacksmith did not answer immediately, and it was evident that he had thought of the same question before. Finally he said, "You see the raw iron that I have here to make into horses' shoes? You know what I do with it? I take a piece and heat it in the fire until it is red, almost white with heat. Then I hammer it unmercifully to shape it, as I know it should be shaped. Then I plunge it into a pail of cold water to temper it. Then I heat it again and hammer it some more. And this I do until it is finished."

"But sometimes I find a piece of iron that won't stand up under this treatment. The heat and the hammering and the cold water are too much for it. I don't know why it fails, but I know it will never make a good horseshoe." He pointed to a heap of scrap iron that was near the door of his shop. "When I get a piece that cannot take the shape and temper, I throw it out on the scrap heap. It will never be good for anything."

He went on, "I know that God has been holding me through the fires of affliction, and I have felt the hammer of experience upon me. But I don't mind, I only hope He can bring me to what I should be. And so in all these hard things, my prayer is simply this: Strengthen me in trials, Lord, and don't throw me on the scrap heap."

– ADAPTED FROM LYNELL WATERMAN

A Living House

Imagine yourself [as] a house that God comes in to rebuild. At first, perhaps, you can understand what he is doing. He is getting the drains right and stopping the leaks in the roof; you knew those jobs needed to be done and so you are not surprised.

But soon He starts knocking you about in a way that hurts abominably, and does not seem to make sense. What on earth is He up to?

He is building a different house than you had planned; throwing out a new wing here, putting on an extra floor there, running up towers, and making courtyards.

You thought you were going to be a little cottage; but He is building a palace.

– C.S. LEWIS (AFTER GEORGE MACDONALD)

A More Difficult Life

When trials and hardships are tossed in your path
    and challenges clutter the way,
When people despise you for what you believe
    and hate you for things that you say,
When the world is unkind and nothing seems fair,
When people desert you and don't seem to care,
You're required to do so much more than your share.
Grow up a bit, climb out of your pit,
    and think what the Lord had to bear.

– ELDER JASON BEYLER

Abraham Lincoln

There was a man whose biography reads in part
something like this:

Failed in business	1831
Defeated for the Legislature	1832
Failed in business again	1833
Elected to Legislature	1834
Defeated for Elector	1840
Defeated for Congress	1843
Elected to Congress	1846
Defeated for Congress	1848
Defeated for Senate	1855
Defeated for Vice President	1856
Defeated for Senate	1858

This was Abraham Lincoln's background when
he won the presidential race of 1860. He was no
shining star on the political horizon, and was far
better acquainted with defeat than victory. He
wasn't even the "people's choice" in 1860. In that
election, he received less than 40% of the
popular vote.

– DESERET NEWS, FEBRUARY 10, 1962

The North Side

A shipbuilding company had this statement in its advertisement: "All of our timber comes from the north side of the mountain." Why the north side? What does that have to do with timber? After investigation, I found out that the best timber grows on the north side of the mountain because of the rigors of Mother Nature. The snow is deeper and the cold is colder, the winds are stiffer, and the sun is not as warm as on the south side of the mountain. The harshness of the weather is a contributing factor to the toughness of the timber.

Human character is not much different from timber. Often the best in personality grows on the north side of the mountain. We grumble about our hardships and difficulties, yet those difficulties help us to grow and become mature. Each of us can look at our lives and see that the times when we made the greatest personal progress were probably when we were living on "the north side of the mountain."

– AUTHOR UNKNOWN

A Missionary's Gethsemane

You're on a mission and things seem tough;
Doors are slammed with voices gruff;
Your companion refused to do his share
You feel discouraged and even despair.
You question your testimony and belief in God;
You wonder about the path you've trod.
Memories of pleasure dance in your brain;
A siren's song, an old refrain;
"The work is hard," and with a taunt,
Whispers, "Not as He wills but as you want."
You tire of rules and feet worn to the bone,
And suddenly decide you want to go home.
You'll never know if you say goodbye,
What might happen if you stay and try,
To follow the rules and do your best,
To serve the Lord and pass your test.
Where do you think that you would be,
If Christ, In the Garden of Gethsemane;
His soul in torment, a trial of fire.
Had selected not duty before desire?

He set the pattern for you and me,
to meet our own Gethsemane.
From boy, to man, to Elder with fire,
Comes only when duty can master desire.

– BERNARD J. BARNES

Friendly Obstacles

For every hill I've tried to climb,
For every stone that bruised my feet,
For all the blood and sweat and grime,
For blinding storms and burning heat,
My heart sings but a grateful song
These are the things that made me strong!

For all the heartaches and the tears,
For all the anguish and pain,
For gloomy days and fruitless years,
And for the hopes that lived in vain,
I do give thanks, for now I know
These were the things that helped me grow!

'Tis not the softer things in life
That stimulate man's will to strive;
But bleak adversity and strife
Do most to keep man's will alive.
O'er rose-strewn paths the weaklings creep,
But brave hearts dare to climb the steep.

– AUTHOR UNKNOWN

The Race

"Quit! Give up! You're beaten!"
They shout at me and plead.
There's just too much against you now.
This time you can't succeed!

And as I start to hang my head
In front of failure's face
My downward fall is broken by
The memory of a race.

And hope refills my weakened will
As I recall that scene
For just the thought of that short race
Rejuvenates my being.

A children's race; young boys, young men
How I remember well.
Excitement, sure! But also fear.
It wasn't hard to tell.

They all lined up so full of hope
Each thought to win that race.
Or tie for first, or if not that
At least take second place.

And fathers watched from off the side,
Each cheering for his son.
And each boy hoped to show his dad
That he would be the one.

The whistle blew and off they went
Young hearts and hopes afire.
To win and be the hero there
Was each young boy's desire.

And one boy in particular
Whose dad was in the crowd
Was running near the lead and thought,
My dad will be so proud!

But as they speeded down the field
Across a shallow dip.
The little boy, who thought to win,
Lost his step and slipped.

Trying hard to catch himself
His hands flew out to brace,
And, mid the laughter of the crowd,
He fell flat on his face.

So down he fell, and with him hope.
He couldn't win it now.
Embarrassed, sad, he only wished
To disappear somehow.

But as he fell, his dad stood up
And showed his anxious face
That to the boy so clearly said;
Get up and win the race!

He quickly rose, no damage done.
Behind a bit, that's all
And ran with all his mind and might
To make up for his fall.

So anxious to restore himself
To catch up and win,
His mind went faster than his legs;
He slipped and fell again.

He wished that he had quit before
with only one disgrace
I'm hopeless as a runner, now.
I shouldn't try to race.

But in the laughing crowd he searched
And found his father's face,
That steady look that said again,
Get up and win the race.

So up he jumped to try again
Ten yards behind the last
If I'm to gain those yards, he thought,
I've got to move real fast.

Exerting everything he had,
He regained eight of ten
But trying hard to catch the lead
He slipped and fell again.

Defeated! He lay there silently
A tear dropped from his eye
There's no sense running anymore.
Three strikes; I'm out. Why try?

The will to rise had disappeared.
All hope had flown away.
So far behind; so error prone—
A loser all the way.

I've lost, so what's the use, he thought.
I'll live with my disgrace.
But then he thought about his dad,
whom soon he'd have to face.

Get up, an echo sounded low,
Get up and take your place.
You were not meant for failure here,
Get up and win the race.

With borrowed will, get up, it said.
You haven't lost at all.
For winning is no more than this:
To rise each time you fall.

So up he rose to run once more
And, with a new commit,
He resolved that win or lose
At least he wouldn't quit.

So far behind the others now,
The most he'd ever been,
Still he gave it all he had;
He ran as though to win.

Three times he'd fallen, stumbling,
Three times he rose again.
Too far behind to hope to win,
He still ran to the end.

They cheered the winning runner
As he crossed the line first place,
Head high, and proud, and happy—
No falling; no disgrace.

But when the fallen youngster
Crossed the line last place,
The crowd gave him the greater cheer
For finishing the race.

And even though he came in last
With head bowed low, unproud,
You would have thought he won the race,
To listen to the crowd.

And to his dad he sadly said,
I didn't do so well.
To me, you won, his father said.
You rose each time you fell.

And now when things seem dark and hard
And difficult to face,
The memory of that little boy
Helps me in my race.

For all of life is like that race,
With ups and downs and all,
And all you have to do to win
Is rise each time you fall.

"Quit! Give up! You're beaten!"
They still shout in my face.
But another voice within me says
Get up and win the race!

– DELBERT L. GROBERG

A Hard Life

Many years ago in Cornwall there was a preacher named Billy Bray. He was a man of powerful spiritual gifts who came out of a hard life in the tin works of England. When he heard someone telling a long story about troubles and sorrows, his remark was: "I've had my trials and troubles. The Lord has given me both vinegar and honey, but He has given me the vinegar with a teaspoon and the honey with a ladle."

– NORMAN VINCENT PEALE

The Spider

King Robert the Bruce of Scotland, pursued after defeat in battle, hid in a lonely cave. He tried to plan for the future, but had lost heart and had decided to give up. Then he saw a spider. The insect was carefully and painfully making its way up a slender thread to its web in the corner above. The king watched as it made several unsuccessful attempts, and thought, as it fell back to the bottom again and again, how it typified his own efforts. Then at last the spider made it! The king took courage and persevered and the example of the spider brought reward.

– ANTHONY P. CASTLE

Zirker's Pine Trees

In 1960 when I was first married, we purchased a home on many acres of land. The first thing we did was plant trees to beautify and add value to the property. I planted trees on every part of the farm that was not conducive to row cropping. There was a good place for apple trees, pear trees, cherry trees, apricot trees, and pine trees. The most beautiful of the pine trees, yet the slowest growing was the blue spruce. I could not afford large trees so all were seedlings.

One of the boundaries was along a two hundred foot cement ditch that carried water for row cropping. It was quite a chore to water the seedling trees when they were young. They needed water at least two times a week so I decided to punch a little hole about the size of a ten-penny nail—one for each of the twenty-five trees along the cement ditch. The water dripped constantly and supplied them with moisture automatically.

As the years went by, the trees grew—especially the trees along the ditch, because of their constant supply of water. I was really proud of this line of trees. They grew faster than the others and looked like they were stronger. Some of the trees that were a little hard to get at looked a little straggly and seemed to suffer, but I kept watering them. The trees were a constant point of personal pride to me—especially now that our home is surrounded by a beautiful forest.

A few years ago, however, I was startled to see one of the beautiful trees along my cement ditch fall over in a strong wind. I was a little concerned and surprised, as I thought that a twenty-five year old pine tree should have a large root system. When a second one fell over in another storm, I began to worry that one of them would fall and hurt someone or destroy one of my nearby buildings. I was curious as to why they couldn't withstand the wind. After some investigation I discovered the trees along the ditch did not have a good root system. The trees were as large or larger than the other pines but their root system was less than half.

During those early years, they had plenty of water and did not have to work hard to put down a root system for support, and did not develop the roots necessary for an adult tree to survive in a strong wind. I eventually cut most of them down and plugged up the water holes. It has been 7 years since I shut off the constant drip water. As of this writing, the remaining trees along the ditch are still standing. Hopefully the root system has grown larger and deeper and can now give the necessary support when a strong wind blows.

Ironically, I have not lost one of the pine trees that struggled early. They look as beautiful and tall today as the other pine trees. The early struggle they suffered was to their benefit and mine.

– RONALD J. ZIRKER

Teamwork

In America in the 1850's, when covered wagons were heading west, the leaders always dreaded the fording of the Platte River. The current was so changeable in the broad, muddy stream that not even experienced scouts could tell where the pockets of quicksand and potholes lay. When an ox- team got stuck, the wagon was usually overturned, dumping family and possessions into the river.

The problem was overcome with some ingenuity and teamwork. When a large number of wagons arrived at the river, the oxen from all of them were hitched together in a long line to pull each of the families across one at a time. Even though one team in the long line might flounder, there were always enough on sure footing to keep the wagon on the move and upright.

– ANTHONY P. CASTLE

PRAYER

Prayer is the key that unlocks every door of difficulty.
But a key is not to be used only once a day;
it is to be used every time you come to a locked door.
– GEORGE B. TULLIDGE

Pray always, lest you enter into temptation and
lose your reward.
– D&C 31:12

The Difference

I got up early one morning
and rushed into the day;
I had so much to accomplish,
I didn't have time to pray.

Problems just tumbled about me,
and heavier came each task.
"Why doesn't God help me?" I wondered.
He said, "You didn't ask."

I wanted to see joy and beauty,
but the day toiled on, gray and bleak;
I wondered why God didn't show me.
He said, "You didn't seek."

I tried to come into God's presence;
I used all my keys at the lock.
God gently and lovingly chided,
"My child, you didn't knock."

I woke up early this morning,
and paused before entering the day;
I had so much to accomplish
that I had to take time to pray.

– AUTHOR UNKNOWN

I Knelt to Pray

I knelt to pray as day began
And prayed, "O God, bless every man.
Lift from each weary heart some pain
And let the sick be well again."
And then I rose to meet the day
And thoughtlessly went on my way;
I didn't try to dry a tear
Or take the time a grief to hear.
I took no steps to ease the load
Of hard-pressed travelers on the road;
I didn't even go to see
The sick friend who lives next door to me.
But then again when day was done
I prayed, "O God, bless everyone."
but as I prayed a voice rang clear
Instructing me to think and hear.
"Consult your own heart ere you pray;
What good have you performed today?
God's choicest blessings are bestowed
On those who help him bear the load."

And then I hid my face and cried,
"Forgive me, Lord, for I have lied.
Let me live another day
And I will live it as I pray."

– STERLING W. SILL

Sincere Prayer

Sincere prayer is the heart of a happy and productive life. Prayer strengthens faith. Prayer is the preparation for miracles. Prayer opens the door to eternal happiness. The Father of us all is personal, ever waiting to hear from us, as any loving father would his children. To learn to communicate with Him, to learn to pray effectively, requires diligence and dedication and desire on our part. I wonder sometimes if we are willing to pay the price for an answer from the Lord.

– BISHOP H. BURKE PETERSON, 1973

No Time to Pray?

We may say that our work drives us and that we have not time to pray, hardly time to eat our breakfast. Let the breakfast go, and pray; get down upon your knees and pray until you are filled with the spirit of peace. It matters not whether you or I feel like praying; when the time comes to pray, pray. If we do not feel like it, we should pray until we do.

You will find that those who will wait till the Spirit bids them pray will never pray much on this earth. My doctrine is, it is your duty to pray. If I could not master my mouth, I would my knees and make them bend until my mouth would speak. If the Devil says you cannot pray when you are angry, tell him it's none of his business, and pray until serenity is restored to the mind.

Let no person give up prayer because he has not the spirit of prayer, neither let any earthly circumstance hurry you while in the performance of this important duty.

– BRIGHAM YOUNG

Prayer

I know not by what methods rare,
But this I know:
God answers prayer.
I know that He has given His word
That tells me
Prayer is always heard,
And will be answered soon or late
And so I pray
And calmly wait.
I know not if the blessings sought
Will come just in
The way of thought,
But leave my prayer with Him alone
Whose will is wiser
Than my own,
Assured that He will grant my quest
And send some answer
Far more blessed.

– ELIZA M. HICKOK

Prayers Are Heard

Prayers are heard. Prayers are answered. Heartwarming is the example of the mother in America who prayed for her son's well being as his ship sailed into the bloody cauldron known as the Pacific Theater in World War II. Each morning she would arise from kneeling in prayer and serve as a volunteer on production lines that became lifelines to men in battle. Could it be that a mother's own handiwork might somehow directly affect the life of a loved one? All who knew her and her family cherished the account of her sailor son, Elgin Staples, whose ship went down off Guadalcanal. Staples was swept over the side—but he survived, thanks to a life belt that proved, on later examination, to have been inspected, packed, and stamped back home in Akron, Ohio, by his own mother.

– AUTHOR UNKNOWN

The Rock

A father asked his son to move a large rock. He tugged and pushed, lifted and struggled without success. Some friends were called to help, but together they could not move it. Reluctantly, the son told his father that he could not budge the rock.

"Have you done all you could?" asked the father.

"Yes," said the little boy.

"Have you tried everything?" persisted the father.

"Yes," said the little boy, "I've tried everything."

"No, son, you haven't," replied his father. "You haven't asked me."

Why do so many of us "heirs of God, joint heirs with Christ" fail to go to him, to keep in touch with our Father? He is anxious to help, but He wants us to learn our need for him, to open the door to him. "And therefore," said the prophet, "Will the Lord wait, that he may be gracious unto you, and therefore will he be exalted, that he may have mercy upon you." (Isaiah 30:18)

– MARION D. HANKS, IN CONFERENCE REPORT APRIL 1972

God, Are You There?

I'm way down HERE!
You're way up THERE!
Are You sure You can hear
My faint, faltering prayer?
For I'm so unsure
Of just how to pray.
To tell you the truth, God,
I don't know what to say.
I just know I am lonely
And vaguely disturbed,
Bewildered and restless,
Confused and perturbed . . .
And they tell me that prayer
Helps to quiet the mind
And to unburden the heart
For in stillness we find
A newborn assurance
That SOMEONE DOES CARE
And SOMEONE DOES ANSWER
Each small sincere prayer!

– HELEN STEINER RICE

Prayer

Prayer! I couldn't live without it; I would have died a dozen times if it had not been for my chance to talk things over with God, and gain strength from Him.

How can we know the mind and will of God? How can we know His plan for our daily lives?

I think the best way to arrive at the right decision is to first pray about it, placing it in God's hands. Then sleep on it. The next morning, when you get up, I believe that the first solution that comes to your mind will be the right one—that is, if you have complete confidence in God's guidance. "But let him ask in faith, nothing wavering. For he that wavereth is like a wave of the sea driven with the wind and tossed." (James1: 6) Ask God's help in faith, and your decision will be right. I have found it unwise to make important decisions at the end of the day, when we are weary and tired. But once we have made a decision, we must not look back, like

Lot's wife. We must act then on the faith that
God has given us the answer—and know that
only good will come of it.

– DALE EVANS

The Secret

I met God in the morning
When my day was at its best.
And His presence came like sunrise,
Like a glory in my breast.

All day long the Presence lingered,
All day long He stayed with me,
And we sailed in perfect calmness
O'er a very troubled sea.

Other ships were blown and battered,
Other ships were sore distressed,
But the winds that seemed to drive them
Brought to us a peace and rest.

Then I thought of other mornings,
With a keen remorse of mind,
When I too had loosed the moorings,
With the Presence left behind.

So I think I know the secret,
Learned from many a troubled way:
You must seek Him in the morning
If you want Him through the day!

– RALPH SPAULDING CUSHMAN

Strike the Steel

There was a man who was trying to earn money to go on a mission. He prayed and he prayed to find a job. Finally he was blessed with a job taking out guardrails on the road so that newer and better ones could be constructed. Upon taking the job, he was told he would be paid for the number of guardrails he separated from the cement blocks. His company wanted to recycle the metal, and needed to separate it from its concrete pilings. The young man didn't realize how difficult it would be to remove the hardened cement from the metal.

Day after day he hammered and pounded to break free the metal guardrail. Bit by bit small pieces would break free but he knew that he needed to go faster. He prayed fervently to know how to work more effectively. A tiny voice answered him, "Strike the steel." He didn't pay attention, because he figured God simply wanted him to work harder. He got a solid 9-pound mallet and began to beat the cement with greater fervor, but progress was still frustratingly slow.

He went to Heavenly Father again in prayer and asked the same thing. Again he heard clearly, "Strike the Steel." The young man wasn't sure what that meant, so he figured that he still wasn't working hard enough and he bought a bigger mallet and a railroad spike to chisel at the cement with more strength and accuracy. There was a little more progress but still not enough. Finally, in desperation he knelt and fervently asked Heavenly Father what he should do. Again came the answer, "Strike the Steel."

After pondering the statement, the young man began to hit the steel guardrail instead of the cement. He noticed to his complete astonishment that the cement began to break free of the posts. The tough cement encasements cracked, crumbled, and fell away from the steel posts as his now-powerful mallet strokes reverberated through them. The concrete, once formidable, now fell away like dirt. That day, he freed more rails of cement than he had done the entire summer.

The young man learned that whenever we are doing something and it's not working, we should try a different approach. The answer to his prayer was simple—"Work smarter, not harder."

– AS RETOLD BY KIMBERLY EVANS JONES

PROPHETS

Surely the Lord God will do nothing,
but he revealeth his secret unto his servants
the prophets.

– AMOS 3:7

Joseph Smith

Here is a man who was born in the stark hills of Vermont; who never looked inside a college or high school; who lived in six states, no one of which would own him during his lifetime; who spent months of his life in the vile prisons of that time; who even when he had his freedom, was hunted like a fugitive; who once was covered with tar and feathers and left for dead; who with his followers was driven by irate neighbors from New York to Ohio, from Ohio to Missouri, to Illinois, and who at the age of 38 was shot to death by a mob with painted faces.

Yet this man became mayor of the biggest town in Illinois and the most prominent citizen of the state, the commander of the largest body of trained soldiers outside the Federal Soldiers Army, the founder of cities and universities, and aspired to become President of the United States. He translated a book that has baffled its critics for over 100 years, and today is read more widely than any other volume save the Bible.

On the threshold of an organizing age, he established the most perfect social mechanism in the modern world, and enveloped a religious philosophy that challenges anything of the kind in history for completeness and cohesion, and he set up machinery for an economic system that would take fear out of the hearts of man.

– JOHN HENRY EVANS

His Witness

I honor and revere the name of Joseph Smith. I delight to hear it; I love it. I love his doctrine. What I have received from the Lord, I have received by Joseph Smith; he was the Lord's instrument. If I drop him, I must drop these principles; they have not been revealed, declared, or explained by any other man since the days of the Apostles. . . .

I feel like shouting Hallelujah when I think that I ever knew Joseph Smith, the Prophet whom the Lord raised up and ordained, and to whom He gave keys and power to build up the kingdom of God on earth and sustain it. . . .

Who can justly say aught against Joseph Smith? I was as well acquainted with him as any man. I do not believe that his father and mother knew him any better than I did. I do not think that a man lives on the earth that knew him any better than I did; and I am bold to say that, Jesus Christ excepted, no better man ever lived or does live upon this earth. I am his witness.

– BRIGHAM YOUNG

There is the Light

On one occasion, as a missionary in Tonga, I received word that a missionary was very ill on a somewhat distant island. The weather was threatening, but feeling responsible, and after prayer, we left to investigate the situation. Heavy seas slowed our progress, and it was late afternoon before we arrived. The missionary was indeed very ill. While praying fervently, the impression came to get him to the hospital on the main island, and to do it now!

The weather had deteriorated, but the impression was strong—"Get back now!" There was much concern about the darkness, the storm, and the formidable reef with its extremely narrow opening to the harbor. Some stayed behind; but eight of us boarded the boat back to the main island.

As soon as we reached open seas, the intensity of the storm seemed to increase sevenfold. As the sun sank, my spirit also seemed to sink into the darkness of doubt and apprehension.

As we rolled and tossed closer and closer to the reef, all eyes searched for the light that marked the opening to the harbor. Where was it? Then I heard the chilling sound of waves crashing and chewing against the reef! It was close—too close. Where was the light? Unless we hit the opening exactly, we would be smashed against the reef! It seemed that the elements were bent on our total destruction. Our eyes strained against the blackness, but we could not see the light.

At the height of this panic, I looked at the captain—and there I saw the face of calmness—the ageless face of wisdom and experience—as his eyes penetrated the darkness ahead. Quietly his weather-roughened lips parted, and without moving his gaze and just perceptibly shifting the wheel, he breathed the words, "Ko e Maama e." (There is the light.)

I could not see the light, but the captain could, and I knew he could. Those eyes, long experienced in ocean travel, were not fooled by the madness of the storm—nor were they influenced by the pleadings of those of lesser experience to turn to the left or to the right.

Soon we were in the protected harbor. We were home. Then and only then did we see through the darkness that one small light—exactly where the captain had said it was. Had we waited until we ourselves could see the light we would have been smashed to pieces. But by trusting in those experienced eyes, we lived.

And so the great lesson: There are those who, through years of experience and training, and by virtue of special divine callings, can see clearer and farther than the rest of us, and can and will save us from serious injury or death—both spiritual and physical.

I testify that in our day there is a living prophet whose eyes see the light that can and will save us and the world. When all about us are sinking in darkness and fear and despair, when destruction seems close and the raging fury of men and demons ensnares us in seemingly insolvable problems, listen as he calmly says, "There is the light. This is the way." I testify that he will so guide us safely home if we will but listen and obey.

– ELDER JOHN H. GROBERG
IN GENERAL CONFERENCE, OCTOBER 1976

Follow the Brethren

Some of us suppose that if we were called to a high office in the Church, immediately we would be loyal and dedicated. We would step forward and valiantly commit ourselves to the service. But if you will not be loyal in the small things, you will not be loyal in the large things. If you will not respond to the so-called insignificant or menial tests that need to be performed in the Church and kingdom, there will be no opportunity for service in the so-called greater challenges.

A man who says he will sustain the President of the Church or the General Authorities but cannot sustain his own bishop is deceiving himself. The man who will not sustain the bishop of his ward and the president of his stake will not sustain the President of the Church.

Follow the brethren. In a few days there opens another General Conference of the Church. The servants of the Lord will counsel us. You may listen with anxious ears and hearts, or you may turn that counsel aside. What you shall gain will depend not so much upon their preparation of the messages as upon your preparation for them.

– BOYD K. PACKER

Revelation

A test whereby we can know whether or not revelation is from God:

1. Is it contrary to instruction from a living prophet?
2. Is there anything secret?
3. Does it bring harmony and peace of mind?
4. Does it square with the scriptures?
5. What have you done yourself to ask of the Lord?
6. Are you keeping the commandments?

By answering these questions, you can know by the Spirit whether or not the revelation comes from God.

– AUTHOR UNKNOWN

The First Vision

You know, if I could not accept the First Vision, I do not see how I could be a member of this Church. I do not see any alternative to that, because it is elemental. There are a few people in positions of some importance, who seem to think that the Church is a great social organization. And if that were all it was, I suppose it would be worth belonging to, but the Church is far more. The social activity, the economic set-up of the Church is important, but without the First Vision and all that flows from it, the Church as we know it would never have been built, would not now exist, and would be but a memory.

– J. REUBEN CLARK JR.

SCRIPTURES

Search these commandments,
for they are true and faithful,
and the prophecies and promises
which are in them shall all be fulfilled.
– DOCTRINE AND COVENANTS 1:37

The Book of Mormon

There is a book I have read many times, yet each time I read it, I find it engages my interest even more. It is a story of courage, faith, and fortitude, of perseverance, sacrifice, and superhuman accomplishments, of intrigue, of revenge, of disaster, of war, murder, and rapine, of idolatry, of cannibalism, of miracles, visions, and manifestations, of prophecies and their fulfillment.

I found in it life at its best, and at its worst, in ever-changing patterns.

It is a fast-moving story of total life, of opposing ideologies, of monarchies and judgeships and mobocracies. Class distinction is there with its ugliness, race prejudice with its hatefulness, and multiplicity of creeds with their bitter conflicts.

Its story has a vital message to all people. The gentiles will find the history of their past and the potential of their destiny; and the Jewish people, the blueprint of their future.

Archaeologists may be excited as they read of ruins of ancient cities, highways, and buildings;

and there may yet be hidden buried gold and priceless records.

Engineers will learn from this great book that those centuries ago, men erected buildings, temples, and highways with cement, and paved roads that connected city to city and land to land.

The psychologists may find studies in human behavior, the workings of the human mind, and the rationalizing processes whereby men convince themselves that good is bad, and that bad is good. Here they will watch history unfold for thousands of years and see not only episodes in the lives of individuals but causes and effects in a total history of races.

This comprehensive book should be studied by politicians, government leaders, kings, presidents and premiers to see the rise and fall of empires, and the difference between statesmanship and demagoguery.

They will see nations born in war, live in war, deteriorate in war, and die in war through the centuries. They may find answers to problems of capital and labor, of dishonesty, graft and fraud, of dissensions, internal rupture, and civil wars.

This single volume records for historians about twenty-six centuries of stirring life, not generally known even to the must highly trained professors of history. It tells of the ancestries of those whose spectacular monuments are now observed in South and Central America and in the Mexican jungles.

In this wondrous book, ministers and priests can find texts for sermons, and men generally can find final and authoritative answers to difficult questions.

It is the word of God. It is a powerful second witness of Christ. And, certainly, all true believers who love the Redeemer will welcome additional evidence of His divinity.

This inspiring book was never tampered with by unauthorized translators or biased theologians but comes to the world pure and direct from the historian abridgers. The book is not on trial—its readers are.

Here is a scripture as old as creation and as new and vibrant as tomorrow, bridging time and eternity. It is a book of revelations and is a companion to the Bible . . . and agrees in surprising harmony with the Bible in tradition, history, doctrine, and prophecy. . . . The two were written simultaneously on two hemispheres under diverse conditions.

In the final chapter of the book is the never-failing promise that every person who will read the book with a sincere, prayerful desire to know of its divinity shall have the assurance of its truth.

The book of which I speak is the keystone of true religion, a ladder by which one may get near to God by abiding its precepts. It has been named "the most correct of any book on earth."

My beloved friends, I give to you the Book of Mormon. May you read it prayerfully, study it carefully, and receive for yourselves the testimony of its divinity.

– SPENCER W. KIMBALL, CONFERENCE REPORT, APRIL 1963

The Family Bible

Old brother Higgens built a shelf
for the family Bible to rest itself,
Lest a sticky finger or a grimy thumb
should injure the delicate pages some.
He cautioned his children to touch it not,
and there it rested with never a blot,
though the Higgens tribe was a troublesome lot.

His neighbor Miggens built a shelf,
"Come, children," he said, "and help yourself."
Now his Bible is old and ragged and worn
with some of the choicest pages torn
where children have thumbed and fingered and read.
But of the Miggens I've heard it said
that each carries a Bible in his head.

– AUTHOR UNKNOWN

The Atheist

An atheist once said, in speaking of the Bible, that it was quite impossible these days to believe in any book whose author was unknown. A Christian friend asked him if the compiler of the multiplication table was known.

"No," he answered.

'Then, of course, you do not believe in it?'

"Oh yes, I believe in it because it works well," replied the skeptic. "It's true."

"So does the Bible," was the rejoinder, and the skeptic had no answer to make.

– ANTHONY P. CASTLE

The Scriptures

Most people are bothered by those passages in Scriptures that they cannot understand; but as for me, I always noticed that the passages in Scripture that trouble me most are those that I do understand.

– MARK TWAIN